A Hundred Lives Since Then

"...Just one way, you do get back home. You have a boy or a girl of your own and now and then you remember, and you know how they feel, and it's almost the same as if you were your own self again, as young as you could remember."

– James Agee, *A Death in the Family*

A Hundred Lives Since Then

Essays on motherhood, marriage, mortality...and more.

Gail
Rosenblum

NODIN PRESS

We gratefully acknowledge permission to reprint essays which originally appeared in the *Minneapolis Star Tribune, MPLS-St. Paul Magazine, Minnesota Parent* and *Our Kids Magazine*. Gratitude, too, for permission to reprint lines from *A Death in the Family* by James Agee (c) 1957 by the James Agee Trust, renewed (c) 1985 by Mia Agee. Used by permission of Grosset & Dunlap, Inc., a division of Penguin Group (USA) Inc.

ISBN 978-1-935666-19-6

Design and layout: John Toren
Illustrations: Michelle Schwartzbauer

Library of Congress Cataloging-in-Publication Data

Rosenblum, Gail.
A hundred lives since then : essays on motherhood, marriage, mortality, and more / by Gail Rosenblum.
p. cm.
ISBN 978-1-935666-19-6
1. Marriage. 2. Motherhood. 3. Families. I. Title.
HQ503.R67 2011
306.874'3092--dc22

2011000791

Nodin Press, LLC
530 North Third Street
Suite 120
Minneapolis, MN
55401

For Sydney, Noah and Carly Bess,

for whom I count my blessings. One, two, three.

ACKNOWLEDGMENTS

Thanks first and foremost to Nodin Press publisher Norton Stillman, who confirmed for me that the three words a girl of a certain age longs to hear are not, "I love you," but, instead, "Want a contract?" Thank you, Norton, for your enthusiastic response to my writing (topped only by Mother), and your wisdom in assigning to me thoughtful and talented editor John Toren. John, your deft touch has been humbling and gratifying. Thank you Lane Stiles, formerly of Mid-List Press, who connected me to Norton and John.

Thank you to my employer, *Star Tribune*, and specifically, Nancy Barnes, Rene Sanchez, and Bob Schafer, for allowing me to chase this project, and to *Star Tribune* editors, former and current, for turning my words into something worth publishing: Susan Barbieri, Randy Miranda, Connie Nelson, Lee Dean, Sue Wolkerstorfer, Laurie Hertzel and Susie Hopper. Also, thanks to Michele Hodgson, formerly with *MPLS-St. Paul* magazine, Kris Henning, formerly with *Minnesota Parent*, and Nancy Diehl and Judith Lipsett, formerly with *Our Kids Magazine*, who provided me for years with generous real estate inside their pages. Thank you, Stan Turner, for generously sharing your KLBB air-time with me, plus all the water I can drink. Thank you superstar editor, Jeff Cohen, who offered the 23-year-old me an incredible start deep in the heart of Texas. You don't regret it, right?

A book cannot be written without friends and, by friends, I mean people who tell you that they like pretty much everything you write. Of special note, thank you Dana Yugend-Pepper, who actually keeps a file with my writing in it; to Deborah Sugerman, who once insisted that a disastrous column I wrote was a respectable B-plus, thus freeing me from the fetal position to try again another day, and to Team Caffeine, who have cheered me on through the considerable thrills and spills of my writing career.

Kim Ruebush Hager stunned me a year ago when she mailed me the photo of my much-younger self on this book's cover. Childhood friend Kim was studying photography at our Albuquerque high school at the time, and I was more than happy to pose for her, leaning across what I believe is my father's Pontiac Lemans. I looked at that picture of my 16-year-old self and thought, "My God…I've lived a hundred lives since then." A book title was born.

Thank you, Reading Goddess (*www.readinggoddess.com*) teammates (a.k.a. Pamela Johnson, Diane Moore, and the splendid Lorna Landvik) for supporting literacy, women and wine (pick your order).

Thanks to my family, who graciously (bravely?) allow me to ponder their every move in many of the essays that follow. A special thanks to my wise and wickedly funny mother, Estelle Rosenblum; my ex-husband, Barry Davis who shares with us his killer pesto recipe; and my partner, Patrick Twiss, who is probably grateful that he met me long after most of these essays were written.

Finally, thank you to the three brightest stars in my universe: Sydney, Noah, and Carly Bess.

Happy reading.

Contents

IV. FAMILY LIFE

V. BUT SERIOUSLY

VI. Holidays and Holy ... Daze

A Hundred Lives
Since Then

1 Butterfly – Becoming a Writer

Beauty
  Usually
    Tells of
      The butterfly
        Every movement
          Real and
            Filled with
              Life and
                Youth.

Okay, it's incredibly schmaltzy. But I was about 11 when I wrote it, younger than my youngest child is now, and I can still recall the physical exhilaration I felt as I completed it. I leaped up from my bedroom floor with the euphoric realization: "I am a writer!!!" In that moment I knew. I knew what I wanted to do for the rest of my life.

2 Letters from Dad

There's a term in movie-making called a "plot point." It describes what happens when you're going along on life's cruise control...la la la....and suddenly everything changes, sometimes cruelly, in an instant. When I was 29, my dad died. This was my plot point.

A Final Letter to a Father

Dear Dad,

A year has passed since your children placed a collection of greeting cards on the kitchen table, hoping against hope that you would awaken in the morning to read them. But you slipped away in the darkness of the night, determined, I'm sure, to spare us the additional anguish of losing you on Father's Day.

This year there will be no cards at all. Just this, my final letter to you.

For quite some time after your death, I kept reaching into my mailbox expecting to hear from you. From the time I moved away from home years ago, your letters were a constant reassurance in my unpredictable life; funny, newsy missives pounded out regularly on your clunker of a typewriter: Movies to see and to avoid. The latest scandals at the university. Your travels around the globe with Mom. Jay's graduation from law school and his engagement to Debra-on my birthday! Mitch's adventures in Hollywood. Births, deaths and divorces.

Sometimes they contained money I hadn't asked for; somehow you knew.

I kept every letter you wrote to me, thinking that when I was a very old woman I would dust off the boxes and unwrap each one like a precious present; every typewritten sheet chronicling a piece of our family's life and the world as it evolved year after year. How could I have known I'd be reaching into those boxes so soon?

Dec. 10, 1987:

You speak of the year's end with the same exuberance that has always marked your letters. Your students, suffering from predictable "bouts of hysteria and anxiety," are preparing for finals. Holiday invitations are rolling in, and cousins are coming to town to help you bring in the New Year. You wish Barry and me luck as we voyage cross-country to Minnesota, suggesting that we start practicing how to keep warm. "Body heat," you suggest wryly, "is a good first step."

Jan. 12, 1988:

You don't mention the cancer, diagnosed three days before Christmas, until the fourth paragraph. First you ask about life in Siberia...uh...Minnesota, and assure me that I am the best writer of my generation. Of course. Finally you tell me that your oncologist has suggested an experimental treatment program in Arizona. "What the hell?" you say. "I'll try it." In the meantime you insist that life go on normally. You promise me you'll live to 100.

Jan. 22, 1988:

Your sense of humor, thank goodness, is still intact. In addition to the experimental drug, interferon, you report that you're also taking two vitamin A tablets a day. "Vitamin A is the basis of the acne medication Acutane," you explain, "so in addition to helping stop the growth of the tumor, all my zits will clear up."

Feb. 29, 1988:

I learn that you had your hair cut, ran into Connie, brunched with friends, are struggling with your income taxes and have decided to cancel a trip to New York, "because the weather is so unpredictable this time of year." Before closing, you mention that the medication is giving you flu-like symptoms, and you apologize for making so many errors with the typewriter. I hadn't noticed. It's been a rough go, you finally admit, but you're hanging in there. "Wrap up warmly," you lovingly close, "and say your prayers for me."

March 14, 1988:

The tidbits of daily life have been relegated to the final paragraphs. You begin by telling me how grateful you are for every day and how appreciative you have become of the natural things in life. You continue to set goals and feel hopeful. You're looking forward to early retirement. You joke about your weight loss, describing yourself as a "prune face," and assure me that by the time Barry and I arrive at the end of the month, you will have put on some pounds. I send ahead a six-pack of a high-calorie, liquid-protein drink in coffee, your favorite flavor. I am beginning to feel helpless.

April 7, 1988:

You and Mom are looking forward to visiting us in Minneapolis. You thank me for understanding that you'd be more comfortable in a hotel. You've begun to clean out your massive collection of office files in anticipation of retirement, although it's a major project that you plan to work on all summer. All summer, you say, and I rejoice. How dramatically my perspective has changed. Just three months ago, I feared you wouldn't be able to keep your promise of living to 100. Today I pray that you'll be here to see the leaves change from green to gold in September.

I set down your letter, and my mind is flooded with memories. My father, whose sweet voice sang me to sleep as a child, who accompanied me on my 5 a.m. paper route without a single grumble, taught me French, coached me through adolescence and addressed all 200 invitations to my wedding ... what would my world be like without you in it?

May 23, 1988:

Your weakening hand has drawn my name and address on the envelope, using liquid paper to cover up your mistakes. I slowly open the flap and stare blankly at words running together and misspellings that you—always a stickler for correct grammar—have tried diligently to correct. "This typewriter is slowly breaking down," you explain. "We really need to think about buying a word processor." For one precious moment, I feel euphoric: You are going to get well! You are going to buy a word processor! But your closing words jerk me back to reality.

"Stay well, happy and no sad songs for me," you write. "And when you think of me, smile."

7

A week later I realize that there will never be another letter. I pick up the telephone and hear your voice, asking me to come home.

A year has passed since your death on Father's Day Eve, June 18, 1988. At the time I was certain I'd never again be able to walk past the Father's Day cards in the grocery store without falling apart. But a week ago, I found myself browsing through hundreds of them, the silly, the serious, the sentimental, and I had no trouble buying one. It was for Barry, your devoted son-in-law, who became a father less than two months ago.

And so the cycle continues. Birth, death, then the wonder and magic of birth again. But as my role shifts from child to parent, I realize that no one will ever replace you—my father of abundant humor, courage and grace—or your wonderful letters that blanketed me in warmth and documented my world until my twenty-ninth year of life.

Rest peacefully, Dad, and know that when I think of you on this Father's Day, and on every other day, there will be no sad songs. Only smiles.

Your loving daughter,
Gail

3 Table for Five

Eleven years after my dad died, my mom got cancer, (yep, another plot point) but she's doing great. Still, I decided at age 39 that I would no longer be so concerned about whether the things I did made sense. I haven't regretted it.

Carly Bess, our third and final child, flew into this world at an hour past midnight on my husband's birthday—a perfect package with a lusty cry and a reminder to me, who felt certain my entire pregnancy that she was a *he*, to continue abstaining from racetracks and Powerball. Seconds later, my emotional hubby rushed out to the waiting area and brought in our exhausted but dazzled older children, who found it difficult to contain their exuberance as they gazed upon their beautiful newborn sister for the first time.

I'm lying.

"Eeeewwww" was about all my horrified 9-year-old daughter could muster, having wished for a sister until she laid eyes on the squawking, blood- and vernix-covered personage who'd be sharing a room with her in the not too distant future. Needless to say, she declined to assist in cutting the umbilical cord.

Our 6½-year-old son offered a more specific review: "She looks like a pig who's been eating in the mud."

So much for magical moments.

Fortunately, after a decent night's sleep, our children's encounter with Carly Bess the following morning was love at, well, *second* sight.

Carly Bess's arrival in this world was a long, *long* time coming.

I couldn't have been more than 12 when, setting the dinner table one evening, I realized that the perfect family size equaled two parents and three children. Five forks. Psychoanalysis would be unnecessary here; this brainstorm most likely occurred because *I* was one of three children, sandwiched between an older and a younger brother who, when not teasing me mercilessly about my training bra, were terrific companions. (Still are).

In my twenties I never wavered from my three-child resolve, testing it out on potential boyfriends who would shift nervously in their chairs and admit that they were having a hard time just trying to decide what movie we should see. After marrying and entering my thirties, I became the mother of two healthy, energetic, wonderful children, and I couldn't have been more grateful. And yet I would often catch myself setting *our* dinner table with five forks—still waiting, I guess, for that additional someone to arrive to make our table, and my life, complete.

But one day I looked up and realized that we had two children old enough to catch the school bus by themselves, plus a home-based business that was eating up our time, plus a laundry list of good reasons to keep moving forward. We were too old for another baby. Our house was too small. Our two kids were merrily on their way into serious childhood. We were finally free of child-care costs, diapers, projectile vomiting. We could subscribe to the *Times* and actually read it. And we'd never, ever have to watch the Teletubbies again.

So what was wrong with me? Why couldn't I let it go? How could I admit to friends agonizing over infertility or multiple miscarriages that I longed for a third? Besides, didn't I know the planet was overpopulated? I had a boy and a girl. We had replaced ourselves. Congratulations. Move on, already.

Move on?

That's when it hit me, the reason for my obstinacy. For the first time in my life I didn't want to move on. I kept thinking about those pop psychology tests that appear in women's magazines: *Are you the kind of person who most often lives in the past, the present, or the future?*

The answer had always been the future. Setting the table at 12, I dreamed of being 18 and setting up my own apartment. When I was 20, I couldn't wait to ditch my apartment and live in Europe. At 23, living in Europe, I couldn't wait to be 25 and secure in my first journalism job. As a newspaper reporter of 25, I couldn't wait to...you get the idea.

Of course I lived in the future. Didn't everybody?

But suddenly here I was, barreling toward 40 and doing everything I could to keep the future out of my happy little life. It wasn't independence or the French countryside or a regular paycheck in my chosen profession that had increased my desire to stay put. Nor was it aging parents or El Niño. It was children.

And nothing but children could keep me here, in this life of surprisingly simple delights: macaroni art and peanut-butter sandwiches. Halloween costumes. Birthday parties. A new bike. *Charlotte's Web*. Only children could teach an adult like me how to live completely in the moment, where even offenses such as the theft of a sandbox toy are immediately forgiven (as long as the toy is returned promptly) and the future is only as far as the next snack. Of course we live in the present. Doesn't everybody?

That third child became more than the fulfillment of a 12-year-old's dream, more than an excuse to finally do the home addition. It became my last chance to restart the clock and hold on to the immediacy of this rich, full life of child-rearing just a little longer. Hubby was on the fence. It was up to me. And I knew what I wanted even if it did include a nauseating year or two with Teletubbies named Tinky, Winky, Dipsy, Laa-Laa and Po.

Still, the practical side of my brain fought me. "Children!" it barked, reminding me of a line spoken by the crusty single male in *Jurassic Park*: "They're noisy. They're messy. They're expensive. They smell."

I barked back: *Popsicles! Lemonade stands! Valentines made out of doilies! A child's soft lips against your cheek...*

"They lose you in shopping malls until you're climbing out of your skin with fear. They break your best stuff. They say things like, 'When I grow up, I'll be a better parent than you.'"

That first smile. That first word. A lost tooth. Monkey bars. Tree houses.

"They lie. They tell the truth. They become teenagers. With nose rings! Who needs it?!"

Well, *I* needed it. Because that paralyzing fear of losing sight of them reminds me of the intensity of love that's possible for another human being. Because broken china doesn't mean a damn thing when measured against a child's broken heart. Because what else could we spend our money on that would mature so perfectly in 18 years (OK, maybe 25)? Because there is nothing in the world as sweet as the smell of an infant's head after her very first bath. I needed that. One more time.

When Carly Bess finally came to us at one hour past midnight on her father's birthday, screaming into the light and noise and commotion of many outstretched arms, I felt immeasurably grateful that we are not always practical people. The future will find me soon enough. Today, though, I contentedly set my table for five and count my blessings.

One. Two. Three.

4 One Hour a Week

In the midst of a very active family life, I also discovered the cure for the envy, self-absorption, boredom and self-pity that more than occasionally crept into my waking hours—in a word, I learned to get over myself.

William waits for me in front of Room 210, hands holding something behind his back, head tilted away as I approach. "I don't feel like reading today," he announces, avoiding eye contact. He is almost 10, handsome and polite, with dark brown eyes as big as pennies. And he's on to me. As the year moves along, he's figured out that I'm a pushover.

"How about one book?" I suggest, "in our favorite spot? Then we can play your game." Negotiations complete, he pulls the board game front and center, and we walk down five steps to a white window seat to begin reading *Frog and Toad Together*. Suddenly, he stops.

"Too many pages," he says. "I can't read that many pages."

"How about if you read one, then I read one. I'll start."

"No," Williams says. "I'll start."

And so it goes. Once a week for one hour, going on three years, William and I meet with the assigned task of improving his literacy. Mostly we goof around. On his high-energy days, we whip through Easy Readers. I celebrate every new word he masters with cheerleader-like frenzy. "Wonderful! Great! You are a reader, William!" He fires back with enthusiasm of his own: "How many books can we read today? Ten? Twelve? Let's read eighteen!"

Sometimes we just play games—Trouble or Mancala. He plays to win, and does. Sometimes, we sneak into the school cafeteria, scouring it for a Popsicle or bag of salty chips. Other days are a chore. He's distracted, annoyed even, watching his buddies swat each other's heads at they march down the hall to the Media Center while he's stuck with me. "William," I tease, "where are you?" On those days, I feel defeated. But I'm never sorry I come.

Once William arrived at school with a family crisis embedded in his face. As we sat together on the white bench, he shed his bravado and tucked wet eyes into my shoulder and I would have held him there forever. But he is, after all, 9 years old. The storm passed quickly. He sat up, wiped his eyes and asked, "Can we play Trouble?"

A teacher I know stopped me in the hall one day to ask if I'd be returning in the fall. Of course, I told her. "Well, good," she said. "William needs you." I wanted to correct her. Actually, I need William.

I am 43 years old, with a full-time newspaper job I like and three neat kids who, so far, still like me. But sometimes I catch myself letting work problems distract me from them at home, when I open the mail instead of focusing on a detail of their day, or rush through their bedtime rituals so I can crawl into bed with a book.

Sixteen years into marriage, I'm a decent spouse. But the most romantic getaway we have these days is to the wholesale club to buy in bulk. At work, where I manage nine creative people, most days go well. But last week I missed a deadline and screwed up an administrative detail and got some facts wrong in a meeting and wondered why they ever hired me.

I have friends I adore who complete my world. But we can never seem to find time for lunch anymore; one is battling depression and my words, meant to comfort, come out trite and patronizing. "Hang in there," I tell her. "It will get better." Dear God.

My world is safe and solid and good—except when the wheels come off unexpectedly and I find myself drowning in self-doubt. Or when I say something stupid, or feel envy, or bark at my kids because I'm tired, or forget to call my mother, or go to work with graham crackers ground into my shoulder and my sweater buttoned wrong.

But I have one hour.

One hour a week when I have no self-doubt. When I walk down a noisy elementary school hallway covered with children's art and my respite awaits me.

"When will you come back?" William asks.

"Next Thursday, silly. I always come on Thursday."

"I wish you could come on Mondays instead," he says. "Then I wouldn't have to wait so long for you."

One hour a week I am granted the greatest reward possible. The comfort of knowing that I am absolutely in the right place, doing the right thing. My life will catch up with me soon enough. But for the moment, it will just have to wait.

5 Un-Married

At 50, I decided to write this book. One essay still needed to be written. Here it is.

My house guests are calling me a freak. They're laughing as they say it and I'm laughing, too, because I knew it was coming and, frankly, I've been called worse. I just told them about my evening's dinner plans and they can't get their heads around why I'd want to spend Friday night at the home of a happily married man and his three kids, whose wife, by the way, is out of town. "I love his cooking?" I say, hoping the statement, if posed as a question, might encourage empathy on their part, or at least an end to the ribbing.

For years, I've been getting grief from relatives and friends about this guy. He and I talk on the phone several times a week, meet for coffee on occasion (we go Dutch), e-mail and text regularly. He knows and likes my boyfriend; even gave a bicycle to my boyfriend's son. His wife and I buy each other gifts.

I can't tell you exactly when our relationship evolved into the mature and thoroughly enjoyable union it is, only that I dreamed for years of this very thing with this very man. This man whose kids are my kids. Whose house was once my house, too. This man I was married to for 21 years.

I *can* tell you, from my professional life writing about relationships, and my personal life living in the middle of many, that we aren't the only exes navigating this peculiarly pleasant state, once released from the bonds of holy matrimony.

I can tell you, too, that while I have never bought Ritalin from the neighbor boy, (or propositioned him for sex) I might as well have from the reactions I get when sharing the unseemly news that my ex and I get along well, that we live six blocks apart and celebrate holidays and our kids' birthdays together.

That is so weird! Your kids must be so confused! You must secretly want to get back together!

No. No. And really no. What we wanted, actually, was to get on with the tasks of daily living with our imperfect selves, and more important, our precious children's selves, in as few shards as possible. Early on, when our grief was big and ugly and unshakable, we had no idea how to get to this place. Didn't, in fact, know that it existed in the world.

Now that we're here, we're like those obnoxious couples who just returned from a ten-day Alaskan cruise: You HAVE to experience it for yourselves!

I can hear you out there screaming. You will NEVER EVER !! give that bastard the satisfaction. And I am here to push back. I am here to tell you that it may take months—or years—and many co-pays to a baseball team of therapists. But, if you can get to the other side, you will breathe more deeply than you have in years. You will be able to focus on what matters, what you really want, always wanted, from your life going forward. Your children will be far better off. Your whites will be whiter, too.

* * *

A story: I'm standing in front of my open refrigerator, studying the possibilities. I am now living in an arrangement known as "bird-nesting." This is when a married couple, too frightened and confused to fully pull the plug, decides to separate, but still has one ounce of wherewithal left to keep the kids' needs front and center. Instead of moving them from hysterical house to hysterical house, the parents move in and out of the family home and, in our case, a one-bedroom condo a few blocks away.

We've been at this for months, experimenting with not being a union. Tonight, though, I know it's over. I know it's over because of the plump piece of salmon, seasoned with rosemary and olive oil, wrapped in plastic on one of the nifty glass plates we purchased in a hurry from IKEA to set up this second home. In theory, our deal is that we move in and out of this condo like members of the Cat in the Hat team. You'd never know either of us had been here. In practice, he forgot to clean up. Hence, the salmon. My ex has a lot of fine qualities, in addition to the ones that tempted me to kill him, but the one I miss most is his  ability to cook like Bobby Flay. Apparently, he's cooking for someone else now.

The million-dollar question is: Am I going to be a Big Girl and eat it anyway? I promise to answer that, but first, a brief history of how we got here.

* * *

We met on a blind date and married on the late side (I was nearly 27, he was 31), ready to commit, eager to start a family. We were good people from good families with similar religious upbringings. But looking back, I realize that the noise between us began even before marriage, a low rumble we ignored effectively. I needed lots of space. He felt abandoned. I was an extrovert who thrived on friends and social engagements. He thrived on ideas, preferring to stay home to create, fix, think. I couldn't balance my checkbook and, recklessly, didn't care. He had an advanced degree in finance and cared very much.

We carried on. Kids keep couples busy. Jobs keep couples busy. Societal and familial pressures keep couples busy, and married, too.

As our three children grew older, the rumble grew to a roar. We were fighting all the time, exhausting each other. But we refused to say the D word. Instead, we began a painstaking journey to save our marriage because we were going to save our marriage. Maybe we just suffered from lousy communication. We'd get better! For a year, we carved out two hours every Sunday to practice the art of talking to one another without feeling small and bad, filling notebooks with Harville Hendrix-y dialogues and 'I' phrases. "When I hear XXX, I feel YYY." Every time we spoke those words, though, the tensions between us grew closer to snapping.

Still, we hung tight, shifted to another strategy. We'd stop expecting so much. All marriages experience libido shifts, job and money stresses, boredom, fantasies about other people... Right?

Eventually, though, even people who knew us best and loved us most were starting to believe that our struggles weren't acute, but chronic. As one of our most perceptive marriage therapists asked us, "Has the milk been out too long?" In other words, how many years can two good people run on emotional empty before somebody tries to fill up elsewhere?

The questions roared inside our heads, accompanied by a constant drum beat: Our kids. Our kids. What about our kids? Ultimately, we decided that staying was riskier than leaving. We needed to end the power struggle and free each other. We knew it, and yet, we cried all the time.

People often tell me that we can have this enviable (and odd) post-marital relationship because each of us wanted to divorce. I respond with a challenge: Imagine a patient who is chronically ill. The patient is, in fact, dying and you know it. But you love this patient with all your heart and for years you do everything you can to keep this patient alive. You seek out the finest experts, no matter the cost. You read every handbook. You try experimental therapies. On the patient's good days, and there are many good days, you celebrate and tell yourselves, "See! It's going to be all right!" Then the patient relapses and you are forced, ultimately, to face the truth.

When the patient dies, I assure you that the grief is no less wrenching, the blame no gentler. On brave days, when I look back at my voluminous journal entries from those dark days, I cannot believe that despondent person was me.

"...instead of my usual "you-fucker" phone call, I just left and cried in my car..."

"...had every anxiety dream in the book last night. Planes crashing. Wounded people..."

"I feel myself getting more and more crazy inside..."

I'm going to bust your other big belief, too: "You can do this because there was no affair." But I do know people, not lots of people, admittedly, but people who do get to this place despite heart-breaking infidelity. It's because they finally understand that the "other person" is rarely the reason. The reason is you and you, who did not know how to love the other in the way he or she longed to be loved.

The marriage of my friend, Max, imploded after his wife confessed to an affair with a co-worker she believed was her soul mate. In the early days, I called him long-distance twice a day to make sure he was getting out of bed. I reminded him to eat but he didn't listen, dropping twenty-five pounds in three weeks. His grief was so thick he could barely breathe through it. "I never wanted to see her again," he said, "but we had this child together."

Slowly, they worked their way back to a civil co-parenting relationship. They moved five blocks apart, threw birthday parties together, even shopped for groceries together on occasion. And over the years what had been merely civil began to seem genuinely pleasant. Today, both are in better-fitting relationships, and they interact like old friends, free of the passion, yes, but of any hint of anger, too. Their son is a well-adjusted, focused teenager keen on, and non-judgmental about, the complexities of human relationships. If I hadn't observed them—seen what they could do—I would never have believed it possible.

The key to getting there is what we tell our kids: Practice, practice, practice. Show up at the soccer game or the wedding of mutual friends (but get a fabulous facial first, if it helps).

Keep your distance. Smile. Then, bolt, have a drink. Next time, sit closer, maybe a row back, smile. Say hello. Then go home and scream into your pillow. I swear to you it does get easier.

The first time we all had Thanksgiving together at the home that was once mine and was now shared by my ex's fiance, I smiled, ate nearly all the sweet potatoes, drank too much and couldn't get out of there fast enough. I still laugh at this journal entry: "For a few days, I wanted to end all the *kumbaya* shit."

It was no easier for her, certain as she was that he and I were going to fall back into each other's arms at any minute (never happened). The first time she saw me pulling up in my car at the house to pick up the kids, she took off running. (She laughs about that now).

Today, I honestly look forward to our extended family gatherings. And that's what we've become. An extended family. It's still awkward at times, and we know that there are boundaries we must never cross. When they announced their engagement, many friends asked me if I would attend the wedding. In fact, my ex asked me if he was supposed to invite me. We could have pulled it off, but why? It was her day. Instead, I hosted family members at my house and listened to my 10-year-old daughter share Every Single Detail, responding with great big oohs! And ahhs! But when my ex's new step-daughter married eight months later, I was among the small number of honored guests. I had a blast, drinking, dancing, sharing their joy. Nothing quite like a family wedding where you don't have to plan or pay for a thing.

We do Thanksgiving and Hanukkah together with everybody's kids. But when I turned 50, I threw myself a big bash with a swing band and fabulous Greek food and told him I wasn't inviting him. Boundaries. He laughed and bought me an expensive bottle of wine.

Sometimes, I still hurt. I wonder why he never drank coffee with me ("Hot, brown water," he called it) but he now owns a fancy coffee maker for their forays with big mugs onto their backyard patio. I wonder when his bad knees that prevented him from running with me turned strong enough to run several times a week with her. Mostly, though, I feel grateful for the bigger stuff, like a son who thanked us at a family holiday dinner because "none of my friends has what I have."

Here's what I think: I think that life is too short to be pissed off forever. That doesn't mean you shouldn't be pissed off at all. I'm all for it. I think you should be so pissed off, or so despondent, that your ribs rattle, you lose sleep, lose your voice from screaming, hate him, long for him, then hate him some more. I think it's fine to have airplane crash fantasies.

But then you need to pick the date when you're going to stop all that. When you stop losing yourself. When you start again to remember who you are and what you want. Now. Going forward. Because holding that grudge forever is "rather like eating rat poison and thinking the rat will die." That's from Pema Chodron's book, *The Places That Scare You*, and it's my favorite quote these days.

The place that scares me most is the sad and lonely place I left inside my soul. I don't plan to return. Yes, I gave up the family home and bought myself a far smaller condo. Yes, I have to be more careful with my money these days, but who doesn't?

The biggest reward is that when I finally was at my best, when I finally knew what kind of love I wanted, I walked into a bar one day to meet a man I'd been fixed up with by that modern matchmaker, Yahoo Personals. We've been together, crazy happy, for four years.

Therapists like to say that marriage has three truths—his, hers, and the one in between. As the years pass, the fog is lifting around that last truth. But there is only clarity about how my ex and I are moving forward. I can still count on the man I spent half my life with.

So, about that salmon.

Yes, I ate it. Mostly. I pulled it out of the fridge, placed it on the counter and chopped it into little pieces. Then I added it to a salad. It was delicious.

I didn't throw it all away. I took the best parts of it and made it mine.

6 Lipstick

In a deluded attempt at self-awareness, I asked my 73-year-old mother, Estelle, and my 16-year-old daughter, Sydney, to comment on me as a mother and daughter. They did.

Gail: What's the one thing I do that drives you both crazy? How could I improve upon it if I wanted to, which I don't?

Mother Estelle: Not hearing from you on the phone. Once each week? Please.

Daughter Sydney: Nagging. You don't do it often, but when you do—like when you nag me to clean my room or return a phone call—it works like reverse psychology. Suddenly, I don't want to do it.

Gail: Communications expert Deborah Tannen says conversations between mothers and daughters can be the best and the worst of everything. Do you both agree?

Estelle: I do.

Gail: That's it, Mom? "I do?"

Estelle: I do.

Sydney: I agree, too. It's such a rush to have a real conversation with you, when we talk about things that matter or when we laugh together. At the same time, though, negative conversations with you make me feel down for longer than negative conversations with anyone else.

Gail: Mom, what's the biggest challenge of having me as your daughter?

Estelle: I'm perplexed when you don't think my very limited suggestions are worth much. You consider every suggestion a criticism. Have you noticed that I don't offer them anymore?

Gail: Um, no. Next question! Sydney, a lot of mothers today want to be their daughter's best friend. Do you wish I did?

Sydney: God, no. I am *so* glad we aren't best friends. I have friends who are buddy-buddy with their mothers and it just doesn't seem right. It's very important that we get along as well as we do, but I also need someone to play the mother role.

Gail: Mom, why do all mothers of your generation say, "Put on a little lipstick. You'll feel better?" What's up with that?

Estelle: Rent a movie with Hollywood glamour stars of the `40s. We all adored these stars of the white-gloves-and-hats era. Bright red lipstick was essential in capturing a man's heart.

Gail: Mom, what's the one thing you want me to understand about you?

Estelle: I'm not that complicated, really.

7 Learning to Text

Some moments are seared into a parent's mind forever. A child's first word. A first step. The first reply from my 15-year-old son when I learned how to text-message him: "U must b kidding me." Hey, he wasn't answering my cell phone calls.

The problem with much of today's technology is that parents of a certain age (me) have no idea how to use it, and kids of a certain age (mine) see no problem with that. But we must fight back, if for no other reason than to perpetuate the illusion that we're still in charge. Or at the very least, that we still know how to play the game.

This is getting progressively harder to pull off. My 8-year-old daughter had to show me (again) how to get from the selection screen on the TV to the specific episode of my favorite DVD reruns. This would have been charming had the DVD not been *Sex and the City*, which she and I refer to as "Friends and the City" because the other, she clarified, is "gross." Thanks, kid. Now, back to bed.

My 17-year-old daughter downloaded dozens of fab iTunes onto the iPod that iGot for my birthday. When the kids aren't around, I stare at that slick black box, the size of my palm, and wonder: How do I turn it on?

I keep a dinosaur of a cell phone in my purse (Razr:

Pretentious! Blue Tooth: Creepy!) mainly because it doesn't ask much of me other than dial and push.

And now, text messaging. I resisted for a long time. I hoped that something new would replace it that didn't require good eyesight or nimble fingers. Then one night I looked up and my two teenagers were leaving by the back door, offering the cryptic teen explainer: "Going out."

When did they discuss plans? Why hadn't I heard the usual chatter from the den? Text messaging. It was time.

My elder daughter, patient as Job, began the tutorial. One push on the cell keypad's number 2 gets A, explained the child who doesn't even look down as her dancing thumbs compose social treatises to friends. Two pushes B, three pushes C, and so forth.

Push "0" for space, "clear" for backspace. Or I could use T9, which predicts words, by pushing the number of the coordinating letter just once. To send a text, push options, then send, find, scroll, select.

Push what??? Push me out a window. Oh. My. God.

I worked and worked until, finally, messages that started like this—xijj u b honf 4 dimmfr?—came out like this: "Will u b home 4 dinner?"

Mostly I got "yep" in return. But it was a start. My kids and I were speaking the same language. Sort of. Sometimes, though, I still resort to Mom's world. For a nanosecond in their high-tech lives, I pull up a stool at the counter where they're doing homework or interrupt them during a commercial break from *Lost*. I bring with me the archaic tools of my trade: a calendar and a pencil. And I ask them face-to-face: "Hey, honey, what's up?"

8 No More "Mommy"

He's already outside the coffee shop, walking toward me on the sidewalk.

"Hey, Mom," he says, nonchalantly. "What are you doing around here?"

I figure I don't need to remind him that I live around here, in the same house, in fact, where he is growing up. Instead, I joke that it's his lucky day. He needed a few extra bucks for an iced chai, so he called me on my cell and sounded surprised that I was in my car, just minutes away.

"I'll bring the money inside," I told him on the phone before I hung up, "so I can say hi to your friends." It works like magic. He flies out the coffee shop door, alone, thanks me for the cash and mumbles something about seeing me later.

"How about a kiss?" I ask as he turns. I hadn't noticed, but now his friends are outside, too. Watching. He offers me the top of his head—a reasonable compromise under the circumstances. Then, a "Bye, Mom," and he bolts.

He's 13, with far better things to do than try to please his mother. But I stand for a minute watching him, taking him in. A child hints in big and little ways that he is doing the good work of growing up. Spending his allowance on iced chais is one example. Size 8½ black Tim Duncan basketball shoes are another. But I wonder how I missed the biggest clue of all.

Watching him cross the street and walk away in the lanky dance of teenage boys, it occurred to me that he will probably never call me "Mommy" again.

F unny thing about the terms of endearment we use. "You aren't going to call me Phyllis, are you?" my almost-mother-in-law asked me in her kitchen a week before my wedding. Actually, that had been my plan. She sensed my embarrassment and leaped in with a gracious save: "Well, there are a lot worse things you could call me." We laughed.

Over the years, I have grown to adore and appreciate her like a second mother. But I've never been able to shift from our compromise, "Mama," the term of endearment used by her grandchildren.

My son came into the world wrapped in his umbilical cord—the first of many unsuccessful attempts to slow him down. He walked at 9 months and rode a bike at 3, spinning around the lake near our house on two tiny wheels like a miniature circus bear.

About that time, I discovered a book by Canadian storyteller Robert Munsch called *Love You Forever*. In it, an adoring mother crawls on her belly toward her newborn son's crib every night, pulling him into her arms to rock him back and forth, back and forth. She continues this nightly ritual as he grows up—first a toddler, then a teen then, even, a grown man—cradling his huge body while he sleeps in her lap. I know. Therapists would have a field day with this scenario, but I still cry every time I read it. Besides, what else could the mother do? He probably started walking to coffee shops after

33

school! And taking the phone upstairs when it rang! And listening to the Red Hot Chili Peppers!

I also have two daughters. I always thought it would be girls who would mystify me as a parent; growing up sandwiched between two brothers, with whom I shared a large bedroom until I was about 10, I didn't think there was anything baffling about boys. Smelly, yes. Baffling? No. I was wrong.

My girls cry about busted-up friendships, then reunite ten minutes later. They laugh loudly, talk fast, and love dollar bins. And they let me know when I annoy them. They *are* me, with smaller hips.

My son is no such animal. He programs my cell phone to read "Moms are cool," then disappears for hours downloading music or shooting hoops with his dad, or playing twelve-bar blues on the piano. He forgets to eat (definitely not his mother's legacy). We talk in short spurts: "Stuffing means blocking, Mom." "I'll be home at six."

I can't help him with his math anymore, and he sure as H. E. double hockey sticks doesn't want me asking him about girls. But once in a while, I'll catch him watching me, taking me in.

Then he'll grin and turn to other things.

Mom. Mommy. Just words, really. Hardly different at all. No more different than a stroller and a ten-speed bike. A first-grade crush and instant messages way past midnight.

Running into my arms after a playground spill and running directly from the court to the fridge for ice.

"I'm fine, Mom," he tells me, blood caking on his knees.

He's right. He really is.

And I'll love him forever, whatever he calls me.

9 Her First Crush

I know his name long before my daughter Sydney whispers it in my ear. In fact, I've known it since he and she were inseparable playmates the summer before first grade. But it wasn't until she agonized over just the right valentine to stuff into his brown bag, until she reported incredulously that classmate Adria was wasting her time pining over Leonardo DiCaprio and Clara was gaga over the Hanson brothers, until she asked me to curl her hair, that the light bulb went on. This special childhood relationship has taken a new twist. My third-grade daughter has developed a crush.

Third grade was the year it happened to me, too. My father took our family on a year-long sabbatical to San Diego and I was the new kid in the classroom. The girls had already sealed their bonds, leaving no opening for me. But a freckle-faced boy named John, looking more like Charlie Brown than Charlie Sheen, took pity on me. We spent the hot afternoons with our feet in the sand or at the nearby 7-11 buying Slurpees. We never touched, but the fact that I can still see his face and recall his name says a lot about how much he meant to me. Boys weren't gross after all. At least, not this one.

Sydney's discovering the same thing. There are the "mean" boys on the bus who warn her away from the back row. There are the boys who win pizza parties for the class when they finally, blessedly, clean out their desks. And there's this one, who illustrates her stories and brings her homework when she's sick and is quietly, sweetly carving out a place in her heart.

My feelings at this development are mixed. Mostly, I'm grateful for its innocence. At 9, my daughter seems light years away from tears, slammed doors, missed curfews and cries of, "You don't understand!" For now, she's simply awakening to something exciting that she doesn't fully understand. And I'm awakening to a humbling new role: her special confidante.

I'm nervous, too, because soon enough I won't be the first person she turns to to share the most intimate details of her life. I just hope I stay in the top ten. So I tell myself: Here's your chance. Tough luck if you're not ready. Give her enough information, but not too much. Tell her that, yes, it's nice to be singled out by a boy, but that she's a complete, worthy person with or without his affections. Nothing to it.

I know that by next week this special boy could be on her gross-out list. Whatever happens, she's put me on notice, reminding me that she's slowly moving out of our grasp and into a bigger world, filled with bigger boys and grander schemes than doing homework together.

And when the right one comes along, I hope she'll remember that her childhood confidante is forever ready to reprise the role.

10 Nothing for Show-and-Tell

Seemed like a fun assignment to me. For the first show-and-tell of the year, all the little kindergartners, including my Noah, were asked to bring in something that began with the first letter of their first name.

"Noah," I asked enthusiastically the Sunday night before school, "what would you like to bring for show-and-tell?"

"I don't want to bring a show-and-tell."

Clearly, I had a problem. Should I insist?

N is for nope. N is also for nudge.

"How about a nickel?" I look around for support. Daddy is clipping his fingernails onto the floor.

N is for nerve.

"I know!" Noah shouts, holding up his hands. "Clip my nails, too! I'll show my nails!"

Weird, but okay.

At breakfast the next morning, Noah looks up at his father.

"Dad," he asks, "where are my nails?"

Daddy looks worried. "Aren't they on your fingers?"

"No. My *nails*. The ones you cut off. I'm taking them to show-and-tell."

N is for nuisance. (See also: Digging through garbage). Daddy gets a bright idea: "How about a napkin?"

No problem. We put the napkin on the kitchen table and leave it there as we drive off to school.

N is for nuts.

"My napkin!" Noah shouts from the back seat. "I left it at home! We have to go back!"

I try to console him. I tell him as calmly as I can that I am really, really sorry, but we can't turn around or we'll never get to school on time. He begs. I comfort. Then wait! I reach into the glove compartment, rifle through the maps and spoons and old suckers.

"Look!" I shout gleefully. "A napkin!"

"It's not a napkin. It's a paper towel."

I take another look. He's right. "It is not," I lie. "It's a very large, sturdy napkin."

N is for neurotic. (See also: Mother).

We arrive at school. I try one more thing: How about if we sneak into the cafeteria and grab a napkin?

N is for "No way."

Fine. I give up. No napkin. No nails. No show-and-tell. What do I care if my child arrives late for school, furious at his mother and unprepared for the only task his lovely teacher asked him to complete? What do I care if other parents strip me of my Mother of the Year title—again?

N is for nonchalant.

I kiss my son good-bye and leave. When I pick him up at the end of the day, he's grinning.

"Ya know show-and-tell?" he asks.

"Uh-huh."

"Well, guess what I brought? Nothing."

"I know, sweetheart."

"No, Mom. Listen. When the teacher asked me what I brought that began with an 'n,' I told her I brought *nothing*. She laughed. She thinks I'm smart."

I laugh, too. N is for nice.

11 Running (Not) to Win

As part of my early training for a midlife crisis, I have taken up running. Wisely, I have found myself a running group that shares my philosophy: "No act of running shall ever be as enjoyable as the act of coffee and high-fat muffins afterward."

Not as wisely, I recently bowed to peer pressure and agreed to compete in an actual race, knowing full well that at the end all I'd get was a cup of sugary replacement drink and little brown rolls with the density of carpet squares.

On the morning of the race, my daughter Sydney looked up from her cereal bowl and asked, "Are you going to win, Mommy?"

"Win, honey?" I wanted to say. "I just hope I come in before the street-sweepers."

"Win, honey?" I did say. "No, I'm not going to win. But I'm so proud of myself that I'm even going to try."

And that's the truth.

When I was growing up, athletic pursuits were synonymous with pain. Not physical pain; I mean the emotional kind. High-jump sticks knocked to the ground. Baskets missed. The awful eternities spent waiting to hear my name called by one side (please, God, *any* side) for a softball game.

I compensated by rejecting the sporting life, filling up

my free time with anything and everything else: student government, music, drama. But I never stopped watching those lithe girls, the ones with the sleek bodies and toned arms, the ones who effortlessly jumped hurdles and ate with a sense of abandon.

I thought about those girls when I came across a recent article promoting the many benefits of keeping our girls healthy during their typically tumultuous teenage years. A girl confident in her body, the article said, tends to be confident in many other areas of her life, too.

But how do we help her get there? When it comes to role models, we Moms may be their best hope. If we enjoy physical activity, they probably will, too.

So there I was, nearing the end of the race with the street sweepers in hot pursuit, when I spotted Sydney on the sidelines cheering me on with her dad and little brother. I called her to join me. She grabbed my hand, timidly at first, then with growing confidence. And for the first time in nearly an hour, I relaxed, letting her wiry, wondrous little body pull me effortlessly across the finish line.

Later that day, when life returned to its comforting mundaneness, Sydney's thoughts returned to the race. "Mom," she consoled me. "You know the ones who won? They've just been running longer than you."

I squeezed her hand and smiled. She's right. But there was nobody out there—nobody—who won like I won.

12 Rivals, Friends, Sibs

I was walking with my friend Karen the other day when she asked me the most astonishing question: "Do your children fight?"

"Only when they're awake," I answered. Seems her daughter and son, at the ripe old ages of 10 and 11, had only recently discovered the delicious satisfaction of tormenting one another. What, I wondered, took them so long?

We knew to brace ourselves for the inevitable reality of sibling rivalry the day our son was born. His 2½-year-old sister, with typical dramatic flair, placed a Band-Aid across her forehead and refused to take it off for a week. "Emotionally wounded," my husband surmised. When the Band-Aid did come off, the mantra began: "Take him back to the hobible... take him back to the hobible...take him back..."

It's been getting more interesting since. He pulls down her fort—with her in it. She shares her chewing gum with him by excising a piece only visible under microscope. He cuts in front of her on his bicycle. Just this morning, she moaned from the back seat that I simply had to get her little brother "to stop thinking so much."

I suppose we could have prevented all this if we'd just spaced them "correctly." When I was pregnant with child two, people asked my due date and pronounced the 2½-year

year spread "ideal." Or the worst possible.

I thought about my friends. I have friends with kids thirteen months apart and five years apart. I have friends with twins and step-kids and adopted kids mingling with biological siblings. They're all sneaking behind closed doors to read *Siblings Without Rivalry*.

I've come to believe that what we all need to do is chill. I say this because of a photograph I keep on my dresser (not the Band-Aid shot). It was taken one autumn years ago, during a visit to a local amusement park. Just before the photo was taken, our son, then 2, turned away from the group and, for a brief but frantic moment, thought he was lost. When he turned back tearfully, there was only one person whose comforting arms he sought: his sister's. In the picture she, the wise 4-year-old protector, looks straight into the camera with a confident grin, her arm wrapped tightly around her little brother's shoulders. He leans in, his head tucked into the nape of her neck, his nose red, his eyes still damp but showing visible signs of relief.

I look at that picture a lot. I look at it and remember that there's something far more powerful going on between these siblings than jockeying for center stage. That something is love, and a building of trust so deep and personal that I dare not intervene.

Sibling rivals, my kids? Sometimes. But over the long haul I know—and they know—that they'd be lost without each other.

13 Riding Away

Unlike the other seasons, my summers have always been marked by milestones. As a child, I associated every summer with something new and exciting: Overnight camp, my first trip on an airplane alone, my first kiss. These days, I tend to mark my summers by my children's adventures: Their first lemonade stand, first fishing expedition with their uncle, first crush for her, first sleepover for him.

But no summer stands out more vividly than the summer of the bike lesson.

It would have been difficult enough had it only been my daughter, then 6, who, with the serious countenance of a sumo wrestler, tucked her upper body in towards her handlebars, pushed off, and rode without training wheels around a nearby school parking lot.

But our son, not yet 4, and not one to believe in "can'ts" or gravity, insisted that we remove his training wheels, too. And off he went, riding behind his sibling-idol in massive circles until his face flushed and his little legs gave out.

My husband and I leaned against the railing with friends, shooting video moments and hollering cheers. I tried to hide the fact that this wonderful milestone left me feeling a little bit blue.

I diagnosed my melancholy a few weeks later when a

friend shared with me the difficulties of keeping up with the continual mood swings and demands of her teenage daughter. Until the bike lesson, parenting a teenager seemed light-years away.

That summer, though, I understood better than ever how fast it all moves out of our grasp; a front-pack becomes a stroller becomes a first step becomes a bicycle becomes a plea for the car keys.

The wise parent, I suppose, is the one who casts the boundary net wide enough to create an environment where it's okay for a child to experiment with different roles, make choices, achieve, fail. The wise parent waits patiently for the tiny white flag to appear when the surly kid reaches out for support and comfort in a brief moment of vulnerability.

The summer of the bike lesson gave me my first taste of what that's all about: Two children begging me for help getting started, chiding me for not letting go soon enough, yelling at me to look, crying in frustrating when I look and they fall. Riding away, circling back.

Riding away.

The most glorious accomplishment of my life as a parent will be if I can raise children who make a clean break from me, who go off to prove, as my now 8-year-old daughter tells me during heated moments: "I'll be a better parent than you."

I hope so. But I also hope that when she and her little brother look back on their childhoods, they'll remember them as one heck of a ride.

14 Remodeling at Last

Somewhere between gazing out the window to the line of men at the port-a-potty in our backyard and nearly losing the baby down a gaping hole in the kitchen floor, it occurred to me that I hadn't sufficiently prepared myself for a home renovation. On the other hand, the whole painful mess seemed eerily familiar. Where or when had I experienced these emotional ups and downs before? This panic? This desire to stop the whole process? I know! Labor! I'll bet the authors of *What To Expect When You're Expecting* never imagined that their wisdom could carry over to home remodeling:

The First Phase: Early Labor. The longest and least intense phase of your home remodeling. You love your builders. You love your husband. Negotiations with contractors are mild to moderately strong, with everyone breathing easy. Some women don't even notice the pain of the 10 percent contingency at the bottom of the contract or the fact that the builder has forgotten to include the back porch in the plans. Emotionally, you may feel excitement (my own bathroom!), relief (my own bathroom!), and anticipation. Some women are relaxed and chatty, learning every fascinating fact about their builder's children and how he hopes to send them all to private colleges. You gladly write that first enormous check, using relaxation and distraction techniques to calm yourself.

The Second Phase: Active Labor. This phase is usually shorter than the first. You may experience increasing discomfort with contractors, increasing backache from moving furniture into the garage, and leg discomfort from sleeping on friends' cheap sleeper sofas while your bedroom is gutted. Emotionally, you may feel restless (Will this ever be over?), and your confidence may begin to waver (Who recommended these people again?). You write the second check to the builder but hide it in the Sheetrock and make him find it. If you feel you need some pain relief, don't be afraid to discuss it with your favorite Dairy Queen server.

The Third Phase: Advanced Labor. This is the most exhausting and demanding phase of labor. Your home is a wreck, your children have no clean clothes, the baby is chewing on nails. Emotionally, you may feel vulnerable (Yikes! This was my idea!) and overwhelmed. If you feel the urge to push...your builder out the second-floor window... pant or blow instead.

A New House is Born: You may be experiencing blood-shot eyes, and black-and-blue marks around eyes and cheeks from vigorous pushing to get the builder to finish last-minute projects before you write the final check. Euphoria that these people are (finally!) out of your life and you have the added space you dreamed of for years. And the craziest feeling of all—that, yes, you'd do it all over again.

15 Remodeling: It's Like Giving Birth

My little house is going away. Not disappearing, exactly. Just being renovated, resided and reconfigured with considerably more space for our growing family. After 11 years of winning the award for squeezing the most creative uses out of a 90-year-old, two-bedroom home that probably should have been torn down years ago, our family of five is joining the ranks of remodelers.

I'll admit that the prospect of my own bedroom with an attached bathroom is about the most decadent fantasy I've had in ages. Kitchen cupboards that actually shut are a close second. But I can sense your envy, so I'll stop. Truth is, the long-awaited expansion is a mixed bag for me. As the walls come down, and new ones go up, there's plenty I'll miss.

Bunk beds. Specifically, the bunk beds our older daughter and son have shared for as long as they can remember. I'll miss hearing them whisper to each other from their pillows at night, long after the lights have been turned off. I'll miss the paper-cups-turned-walkie-talkies that hang from top bunk to bottom. I think this forced togetherness is one of the greatest gifts we no longer give our children, as we eagerly seek out homes with separate bedrooms for each child. I chronicle their budding closeness, nurtured by shared drawers and book cases, and I can only assume these years together will serve them well down the road, particularly in marriage.

My crowded bedroom. We jokingly call it the "furniture showroom." One bed, two bedside tables, a vanity, an antique armoire, a bookcase, one oversized dresser, one crib, two laundry baskets, one rocking chair...gee, if there were just more space, I'm sure I'd do my sit-ups every night. But when I need an escape, it is into this cluttered retreat I go, surrounded by so much I hold dear. Because the walls are cracked, I've never paused before tacking up my favorite kids drawings in lieu of "finer" art. Our new bedroom will be a bit on the intimidating size – sparse and clean, with grown-up furniture and plenty of closets to hide all the junk.

My self-cleaning kitchen. OK, it doesn't clean itself. In fact, no human cleans it much, either. But when you have a kitchen this old, a nice thing happens. Decay on the counter becomes part of the charm. A new kitchen brings with it so many responsibilities, like keeping it *looking* like a new kitchen.

Still, this little house has served us well. It's kept us close and spared us from numerous financial and practical challenges. Yes, the increase in living space we'll gain by the renovation will be welcome relief...yet the simplicity of what we left behind can only grow more attractive as it settles into memory and develops the sweet patina of nostalgia.

16 New Hope for the Pot-Luck Impaired

There are many ways to take society's pulse, to find out what really gnaws at people deep within their souls. The titles of best-selling books are a good indicator. Increases in home-schooling or the latest cries of desperation from Wisteria Lane could be others.

But I wonder if anything taps into human anxiety, at least the female variety, as well as what I found in a shopping mailer the other day: The personalized potluck pan.

"Now your pan will always find its way back to you after a potluck!" the offer read. "There won't be any question about who this pan belongs to, because it's etched with your name and any message you choose, up to thirty characters." All this for only $15.99!

I admit that I carry enormous potluck angst, but for perhaps an unusual reason. I cart my pan to parties and pray —pray, mind you—that no one associates it with me.

"Who made this...this...burned noodle thing?" I can hear the hostess inquiring. And I wonder, "Am I paranoid, or is she really looking directly at me?"

Upon deeper reflection, with my hand plunged into a bag of Toll House dark-chocolate morsels (which don't make it into my potluck pan nearly enough), it occurred to me that many of the women in my life would enjoy such a thing.

My mother-in-law, Phyllis, for one. She will arrive at a potluck carrying a casserole she whipped up following a recipe something like this: "Soak two pounds of pinto beans overnight for twenty years. Sauté three onions in the shapes of little stars. Marinate tenderloin in a combination of picante sauce, soy sauce, and a fine cabernet, then lightly bread with homemade crumbs crushed to the consistency of beach sand. Boil, then bake the meat in a clay pot at 375 degrees for forty-eight hours, stirring every thirty minutes. Then brine until Thanksgiving. Spin three times to the right holding a spatula in left hand. Then repeat in opposite direction. Eat and enjoy."

I will inscribe her pan with the name "Mama," and the message: "It was no trouble. Really."

My friend Robin will undoubtedly make something sweet in the new pan I give her. She will use her favorite ingredients: Four pounds of butter (per person), one truckload of sugar, whole cream freshly squeezed from the nearest unsuspecting cow, and three chocolate bars with no less than 70 percent cacao. Her potluck pan will say: "Robin: When's dinner? This IS dinner."

While I'm at it, I might as well buy a personalized pan for myself. Maybe next time, to surprise the hostess, I'll undercook the noodles instead of burning them. Either way, my casserole will carry a salivating message:

"Gail: To the table everyone! The pizza man has arrived!"

17 Finding a Babysitter

I met a woman who, when she moved to town a few years ago, was so desperate for a friend for herself and her young child that she placed a classified ad in the newspaper. It read: "Wanted. A friend." The ad worked, and she and another young mother have been the best of friends ever since.

I decided to do the same for myself. Not to find a friend. To find a babysitter. The ad read like this:

"Wanted: Responsible teen, with a love for three delightful young children, willing to spend occasional Saturday evenings at our home to allow grown-ups to go out for dinner and not have to cut up meat into tiny pieces. A little light housekeeping, such as washing a few dinner dishes and picking up toys. Competitive hourly wage."

Silly me. I should have known that no teenager would respond to an ad like that. Have you tried to get a babysitter lately? These kids have LIVES. They don't want to be stuck reading *Goodnight Moon* to a toddler with a runny nose.

So I revised the ad a bit:

"Wanted: Teen who can deal with three of the world's easiest children for limited time periods, willing to spend occasional Saturday evenings at our home so that grown-ups can go out and wolf down pasta that doesn't come out of a can. A little light housekeeping, such as throwing the leftover pizza box into the garbage can. Competitive hourly wage, plus bonus if the kids are asleep when we get home."

I waited by the phone. It didn't ring. I tried again.

"Wanted: Teen. Doesn't have to like children. They'll stay in their rooms. For occasional Saturday evenings at our home so that grown-ups can walk up the street for a cup of coffee. No clean-up necessary. Friends welcome. Competitive hourly wage, plus use of the car."

Still no response. I was getting desperate. I tried one more time.

"Wanted: Teen. Must know what a child is. For occasional Saturday evenings so that grown-ups can take a shower. No responsibilities. Competitive hourly wage plus use of the car. Heck, keep the car."

Bingo! The phone rang. She introduced herself at Alison. She was 14, soft-spoken and polite. Alison is an A student, loves children, is happy to make dinner, clean up and read *Goodnight Moon* as many times as necessary. She didn't even care how much we paid. She just appreciated the experience. By the way, Alison didn't see the ads. She lives nearby and figured parents with three young children deserved a night out every once in a while.

I hired her, of course. Then hubby and I got dressed quickly and leaped into the car before she could ask for the keys.

18 Handyman

I fell in love with Myron the way many women fall in love with a man. I spotted him across the street, all 6-foot-1, 210 pounds of him, perched on the roof of my neighbor Stephanie's garage. He spent the whole day up there alone with his nail gun, taking what I calculated to be a five-minute lunch break to eat what I calculated to be a 16-ounce sandwich in his truck. By nightfall, Stephanie had the best-looking garage roof in the neighborhood.

I couldn't stand it.

I marched over, introduced myself and promised Myron a lucrative future in my House of 1,000 Weekend Projects. Soon he was mine. Well, ours. I think my husband was in love with Myron, too. At last, he could stop agonizing over what he never had time to finish and start worshiping someone who did.

We quickly learned a few things about Myron. First, he was a man of very few words.

"How ya doin', Myron?" I'd ask him.

"Good, thanks."

"Been busy?"

"Yep."

"Would you like something to drink?"

"Nope, thanks."

While Myron wasn't much in the small-talk department, he excelled in what really mattered. There was nothing he couldn't do. Leaky skylights were sealed, a backyard fence for two little dogs was built in two days. Junk-filled closets became organized living "cubes." Porches gained new paneling from floor to ceiling. A bedroom closet was transformed into a charming sleeping alcove.

If there were such a thing as a giddy-monitor, you could measure Myron's impending arrival at our house by how high the meter climbed.

Myron, of course, would consider this nonsense. Hard work was all he knew.

He grew up on a dairy farm near Catawba, Wis., one of fourteen children of Alice and Joseph Kempen. There was Bardeana, who died at age 10 of brain cancer; Patrick, Mark, Jake, Joann, Myron, and his twin brother, Byron. (Byron, born

first, says Myron pushed him out of the womb. Myron says he couldn't take it any longer.)

Then came Arthur, Luke, Luann, Carla, Janel, Mary (who died at birth) and Tilla.

Together they worked the fields, cleaned the barn, baled hay, tormented and loved one another, attended a small Catholic church, and gave thanks for three hearty meals every day.

Every December, the Kempen children sat at the kitchen table to pick out one gift each from the Sears catalog. If it was a good year, they could spend $10. Tough years, $5. On Christmas morning, there were still chores to do, so they'd head out and return home to find their selections laid out side by side on the table, unwrapped.

Seventh grade was a banner year for Myron. The family got indoor plumbing, and he no longer had to share a bed with Byron. He was a decent student, but he preferred buddies to biology. He spent his free hours cruising in the truck, attending farm auctions and working on roofing jobs with his big brothers. He liked hunting, too. The camaraderie part, not the shooting part. He never brought a gun, preferring to drive the deer.

On Halloween, the Kempen kids knew there would be no trick-or-treating. Alice and Joseph didn't believe in it. So Myron dressed up in women's clothes and knocked on the door. Alice couldn't help but be amused. "Always Myron," she said. "Yep. Yep. Uh-huh."

Once Alice woke up at 3 a.m. to a driving rain and realized that Joseph wasn't home. Panicked, she went upstairs and asked herself, "Which son am I going to wake up to go find him? Which one could handle the possibility that we could find his father dead?"

Alice and Myron drove slowly along the back roads until they found Joseph, helping a cow give birth in a neighbor's barn.

In his senior year of high school, a guidance counselor told Myron he wasn't college material, and Myron believed him. He signed up for tech school, telling his teacher during the first month that he had a morning job but, really, he was sleeping in. It was a luxury he never had as a kid.

Myron was on the scrawny side, so he started weight-lifting, beefing up at one point from about 150 to 220 and adding "weight-lifter" to his life experiences. He started a moving company, then delivered packages, then sold auto-body supplies—anything he could do with his hands.

Single and living a simple life, he figured about the best thing he could do with his money was share it. Around Christmas in the year Janel started college, her proud big brother sent her a completely unexpected $200. "Enjoy Christmas," he wrote.

Eventually, friends worried that Myron was turning into a bore, so they fixed him up on a blind date. Linda thought he was a nice guy but, oh my, so quiet. She didn't know how she'd manage. On their second date, a New Year's Eve party, she put him to the test, ditching him to watch him mingle with people. He did pretty well. At midnight, though, he just sat there. So Linda kissed him. And that was that.

One month after their wedding at a Lutheran church, on a glorious October day in 2000, Myron was in our unfinished basement, working his magic. He got a call and froze. Then he asked my husband if it would be all right if he took the afternoon off.

A mole under Linda's chin was skin cancer.

"Of course. Go," my worried husband told him. Then he did the only thing that seemed appropriate at the time. He drove to Menards and bought Myron a new nail gun.

Myron came back the next day with more color in his face. The doctor said Linda would be all right.

Not long after, quiet Myron was bursting with a secret. They were expecting. The Christmas before baby Hannah was born, I did something I'd never done. I bought Myron and Linda a Christmas ornament, a simple pink and white rocking horse. Being Jewish, I had no idea if this was OK because I figured that Christmas ornaments were such a personal thing. But I wanted Myron to know how much he meant to us. Linda tells me it was Hannah's first Christmas ornament. Linda calls it "beautiful."

But the most beautiful gift, hands down, arrived at our house soon after.

"Kind of a wet day, eh?"

"So great to see you, Myron. I'll bet Hannah's keeping you very busy."

"Yeah. Yup. They grow quick."

Myron has no big plans for Christmas except to try to understand why Linda makes such a fuss. "Don't buy too much for Hannah," he tells her. No use.

I figure he'll hold his wife tightly and, if he's smart, give her a kiss. Then he'll spend much of the day on the floor with Hannah, playing with a collection of toys the likes of which he never knew as a child.

19 Cabin-Lust

My friend Robin is selling her cabin. You could say that she has every right to do this, but you'd be missing the point: She didn't ask me first.

When she and her husband, Michael, bought this cabin six years ago, (also, for the record, not asking me), my husband and I thought they were nuts. They had jobs and a teenage daughter busy with friends. They had an aging dog named Sprinkles who wanted nothing more than to be set loose in her own back yard to sniff the hosta and lift her graying leg. And they had us, their neighborhood friends, for heaven's sake, who expected to see them when the frenzied work week was over.

Coming from New Mexico, where the only people who lived in cabins ended up on the front page of the *Albuquerque Journal*, bearded and shackled, it seemed to me that buying a cabin was like taking oneself hostage. There would be crazy traffic jams on the way out of the city on Friday afternoons, two mortgages, sand in your shoes and on your floor, ducks quacking at the crack of dawn—not to mention the inevitable sewer problems. Who needed this torture?

Robin, amused at my incredulity, handed me a calendar one morning. No pressure a'tall, she said, but if we were interested, we could pencil in a summer weekend and come on up.

So we went on up.

And we kept going on up.

At Robin's cabin, our older daughter Sydney lost herself for hours in a novel, dangling from a tree swing. Our son Noah, a reluctant swimmer, took his first plunge into the cool lake water, motivated by Robin's firm arm around his waist yanking him in. And our youngest daughter, Carly Bess (Robin's godchild), spent some of her best babyhood hours nestled in Robin's arms in a hammock just feet from the water's edge. I think that's why, to this day, she seeks out the rhythm of swings at the playground.

At Robin's cabin, I made my first and only cheesecake—something I would never have the patience or time to do at home. Robin, the culinary cheerleader, guided me through every step, not flinching when the recipe called for lemon zest and I grated my finger instead.

And it was at the cabin that I heard my first loon. It woke me one morning that was really still night, with a moon so white and round and huge I thought it had overtaken the sky.

Without our realizing it, cabin life began to seep into my family's soul. It became an expectation. And while summer was the natural time to make the drive, we took friends up one winter and built roaring fires. Every fall, I headed up for an annual women's weekend, a raucous gathering with as many as ten female friends. We'd drink wine (cheap and expensive were welcomed equally), laugh about weird sleeping habits, and bolt *en masse* to nearby estate sales.

At night, we aging hotties would play Scrabble and watch *Shirley Valentine* on the VCR. In the morning, without planning, we would make our way to the dock one after the other, where there were just enough chairs, just enough breeze, and more than enough coffee and cream. Some mornings no one would speak. Didn't have to.

Those mornings are memories now. Robin is selling her cabin. There's too much noise there, too many newly built cabins on steroids. Too few household projects left for this industrious duo. She and Michael have bought a little fixer-upper about fifteen minutes northeast on a secluded lake called Sand. It's got one bedroom. Her friends are trying not to take that personally.

Robin promises that their plans include adding two more bedrooms; plenty of room for visitors. She knows who will be one of the first to grab the calendar when she passes it around this time: a friend from the Southwest who learned, through her, the joys of solitude and simplicity, the importance of stretching outside one's comfort zone to find new comforts, and the music waves make when caressing bare feet. She knows all those things. And she didn't have to ask.

Robin's One and Only (But Very Good) Cheesecake

Crust:
1 cup sifted flour
¼ cup sugar
1 t. grated lemon peel
½ cup butter
1 slightly beaten egg yolk
¼ t. vanilla

Filling:
5 8-oz pkgs cream cheese
¼ t. vanilla
¾ t. grated lemon peel
1¾ cups sugar
3 T flour
¼ t. salt
4 or 5 eggs
2 egg yolks
¼ cup whipping cream

Make crust:

Combine first 3 ingredients. Cut in butter till mixture is crumbly. Add egg yolk and vanilla. Blend thoroughly. Pat ⅓ of dough on bottom of 9-inch springform pan. [sides removed]. Bake in hot oven at 400° for about 8 minutes or until golden; cool. Attach sides to bottom. Pat remaining dough on sides to height of 1¾ inches.

Make filling:

Let cream cheese stand at room temperature to soften. Beat creamy. Add vanilla and lemon peel. Mix next 3 ingredients, gradually blend into cheese. Add eggs and egg yolks one at a time, beating after each to blend. Gently stir in whipping cream.

Turn into crust-lined pan and bake at 450° for 12 minutes; reduce heat to 300° and bake 55 minutes more. Remove from oven and cool for ½ hour. Then loosen cheesecake from the sides of the pan with spatula and cool for an additional ½ hour. Then remove the sides completely and cool 2 hours longer.

Serves 12

You may have to bake longer than 55 minutes, until it's not jiggly in the center.

20 Our Neighbor's Fence

The fence went up in two days, two hundred cedar slats measuring three feet high, set in a row running up the gently sloping yard toward two corner posts. In a neighborhood where fence construction creates the kind of stir generally reserved for buckthorn removal, we were quickly inundated with oohs and aahs, and a bit of good-natured ribbing.

"You built that big fence for those little dogs?" asked a bemused woman strolling by. Others commented that it was nice to see a "neighborly" fence—the kind built to keep two new pups in without suggesting that humans ought to keep out. The kind of fence that John never would have built.

John lived next door when we moved in sixteen years ago and his fence created quite a stir, too, although nobody shared their opinions about that too loudly. John's fence was chain-link and covered in forbidding vines. It encircled his house, sealing off his driveway and front walk, with signs warning: "No trespassing!" "No soliciting!" Front-yard roses were merely a reminder that John fancied a flower with thorns.

And if that weren't enough to underscore John's need for privacy, he added a Doberman pinscher, a German shepherd, and a Rhodesian ridgeback as exclamation points. One of the dogs was named Frida, as in, "*Frida!ComehereorI'llrip yourlittlelegsoff!*"

In our hasty relocation to the Twin Cities one December, we somehow missed that we were moving next to the neighbor from hell.

My mother, however, caught on quickly. She made John's acquaintance early one spring morning when she set out in our modest garden to pick flowers. "Get away from my fence!" John bellowed through an electric bullhorn from inside his house (although one might question why a man packaged in a 6-foot-6, 350-pound frame needed a bullhorn). My mother bolted into our kitchen, grabbed her newborn granddaughter in her arms and blurted out the only thing that made sense to her at the time: "I'll buy you a house in the suburbs!"

We didn't move, of course. We loved the character and history of our neighborhood, its proximity to lakes and parks. And the other neighbors seemed pleasantly normal. Many had lived on this block for decades.

We vowed that we would stay and evolve, become Neighbors of the Year. We would smile at John (although it was hard to spot him up there on his second-floor deck, built on stilts). Our children, in their innocence, would charm John, open his heart. (Instead, he eyed them suspiciously and called them "little bastards.")

Secretly, we hoped John would get cold and move to Florida. But he stayed, as did we, working and raising our family. When we did share a rare moment of neighborly chatter across The Fence, John would warn us of hidden sinkholes in our backyard, and ask if we knew that our house had been hit by lightning. Twice.

Once, I watched anxiously as John stepped out of his house and headed for . . . ours. He rang the bell. I hesitated before answering. When I did, he presented me with a plateful of freshly baked cookies. I set them on the kitchen counter and my husband walked around them as if they were a crime scene. When he wasn't looking, I ate every one.

Early every morning, John unlocked his gate just long enough to back out his pickup truck, with a huge stuffed lion in the cab, then drove away to his government job. He returned just as predictably.

We never saw anyone but John come or go.

Years passed. John's health declined. For a while we didn't see him at all. I felt guilty wondering if, hoping that, he had finally gone on to his great reward. Then we heard he was in a nursing home after losing three toes to diabetes. Eventually, he lost a leg. He returned home, retrofitted his truck to make it handicap-accessible, and had a ramp built in front for his motorized wheelchair. John was back.

But he was weakening. And one day something notable happened. We came home and a man was helping John in his backyard. The stranger began to appear regularly, mowing, shoveling, shopping, sorting the mail. Who was he? A family member? Dear God? Were there more people like John out there?

But the newcomer turned out to be one of John's co-workers, a decent man who said he learned from John how to adjudicate and how, when his marriage was in trouble, to think clearly and work things through. He was honored to help John, because that's what friends do.

More than stunned, we wondered if we, too, should try a little harder. Cal, who walked by John's house every day for forty years, went inside for the first time to see the computer

John now used to work from home. Mary Lou brought him homemade soup. Mark crossed the street to share cigars (which John insisted were from Castro himself) and even changed John's dressings once when the home health nurse had car trouble.

In the spring of 1998, when I was enormous with my third child, John would ride his wheelchair down his ramp and through his gate as the school bus pulled away. Then he'd catch my eye. We'd talk about sidewalk conditions, tree rot, taxes. I kept waiting for him to shock me with one of his Johnisms. But he never did. I started to worry when I didn't see him.

About a week after my daughter was born that year, I stepped into the July heat and saw strangers in front of John's house. My husband went over and returned with the news: John had fallen the previous Monday. He died alone on his kitchen floor. And I did something I never imagined I would do. I cried.

I never did learn for sure what would make a man so large become so afraid of the world. But the clues I gathered revealed a life neither as exceptional nor as frightening as John might have had us believe.

He was not born in that house, as he liked to say, but in a tiny Iowa town in 1930. His father was a military man-turned-salesman who cried only twice: once when he lost a son during childbirth and a second time when John went into the service. John's mother was a nurse who, every Halloween, dressed up like a witch and presided over a dry-ice cauldron.

John worked as a bouncer to pay his way through college, where he earned a degree in writing. It is believed that he loved a woman once, in Germany, while in the service. It is certain that he loved spicy foods and sweets, rejected packaged bread, and drank his milk whole, mixed with half and half.

He had other soft spots. Rita down the street remembers a long-ago May Day when her daughter, Rachel, was about 6. Rachel's kindergarten teacher told the children to make a May basket for someone "who needed to be happy."

"Mommy," she said. "I want to give it to that big man."

Rita thought, "Oh, God," but she said only, "Of course." So they walked up the street, rang John's bell and presented the unexpected gift. From then on, John never missed an opportunity to smile at Rachel and say hello.

His younger sister, Shirley, told how he gave her money when she got divorced and was reduced to skinning and eating her son's rabbits. John's niece, Marna, didn't care for her uncle, however. He called her "pork chop."

But he was good to his mother, many said, caring for her through her own struggle with diabetes and years of blindness. She died in 1982. Soon after, The Fence went up and the menacing dogs appeared.

"It's sad," someone said later, "that a person lives a whole life in a neighborhood, yet no one really knows him."

"He was trying to lock the world out, ya know?" said another.

After John's death, the house sold quickly to a handsome young couple with a baby and small dog. Not long after, The Fence came down.

But anyone paying attention knew: It already had.

21 The Book Club on My Block

We walk down the street in silence, partly because the bitter night air demands our concentration, and partly because we don't know each other well. Near the end of the block, we move up the front steps of a neighbor's house and go inside, where coffee is brewing and popcorn beckons from overflowing bowls.

I take off my coat, introduce myself. This is only our second gathering, so I'm stumped on most names. But I'll know them all soon. I feel a kinship with these women, and await this monthly gathering with an intensity that might seem peculiar. I'm 40 years old. I have three children, one of them a baby who has no interest in sleeping at night. I have two jobs, great friends, a regular running group and a Wednesday date at my kids' school. I have no time for frivolous endeavors like book clubs.

Welcome to my book club.

I might never have found my way here had it not been for my neighbor Kris. Last fall, she sent out a letter: How would the women on our block like to get together once a month to discuss books? I was intrigued. More than intrigued, I was overjoyed. For one moment, I was back in my childhood neighborhood, running into the street to join a swarm of kids for a game of kickball. Back then, I knew the names of every person in every house on a block that stretched one-quarter of a mile. Both sides.

And here I was, all grown up, moving into my eleventh year on this block, and I could count on one hand the neighbors whose names I knew; ask me to name their kids and I'd be down to about two fingers. The chronic illness of modern life. But Kris was offering a cure. Somehow I'd find time to read the damn books.

One Tuesday night, I packed up the baby and headed across the street for our first meeting. I counted fifteen women, among them a school psychologist and a Teacher of the Year. A resale shop owner and a children's toy store manager. A health care lawyer and a full-time mom and a retiree who spends her winters in the Texas Valley working in an orphanage.

The women on my block. The women in my book group. My missing link.

By the third meeting, I know everyone's name. I learn that Sarah and Rebekah are pregnant. That Felicity has just returned from her native Australia. That Carolyn's younger son is in Belize. Oh, yes, we discuss the book, too.

It's a funny think about books. The best ones take you to places foreign, exotic, uncharted. But my book club takes me to a place I need to be even more. A place ordinary and familiar. As warm as a blanket. And as close as next door.

22 Street Fair

We headed out to one of our favorite annual events last week—a street fair organized and run by neighborhood kids, with proceeds benefiting our local library. There were art activities, baseball cards and used books for sale, and enough homemade cookies to make dinner unnecessary.

But the greatest excitement, aside from discovering that our one-year-old is a petty thief (preferring not to bob for apples but to steal one outright), came courtesy of my good friend Mary. One minute she was wearing jogging shorts and a T-shirt, snapping photos of her two sons and schmoozing with friends. The next minute, she was bouncing out of her house with a baton in her hand, wearing black velvet adorned with golden tassels.

Mary???

The crowd stood in rapt attention as Mary twisted and circled and threw her baton into the air to the pulsating beat of "Rockin' Robin." No one could match her. Not the high school jazz quartet, not the yo-yo hotshot, not even the budding thespians performing "Little Bunny Foo-Foo." I don't know what surprised me more: The fact that Mary actually caught the thing, or that she could still fit into that little spangled outfit she wore in high school.

It got me thinking. Let's say that next year I decide to do something in the talent show that would surprise and delight my friends—something that would make them say, "After all these years, I never knew Gail could do that!" Problem is, nothing came immediately to mind. After mulling it over, I dug up a few possibilities:

I could eat ice cream sandwiches. I'll bet none of my 40-something friends knows that when I was in seventh grade, kids would gather around me to see how many ice cream sandwiches I could eat in lieu of mystery-meat school lunch. My record—seven—was recorded in the weekly school newsletter.

I could sew a dress together in record time—backwards. I take pride in the fact that I was the only girl in my junior high sewing class who sewed the hand-embroidered bodice of her dress inside-out. I explained to my teacher, a humorless woman, that I did so to place it closer to my heart. She flunked me anyway.

I could do the limbo. About the only benefit of being the slowest-to-develop girl in the entire state of New Mexico was the fact that I could dazzle at the limbo way longer than all the other, more pubescent girls who (ha ha) knocked the stick down as soon as their belly cleared it.

Or, I could do what my high school drama teacher taught me was as important a role to play as being the star. I could be a great audience member. As Mary performed, I could clap and hoot just like this year. Then I could head over to the bobbing apples and delight my toddler by grabbing one with my teeth.

23 Gender Guessing

Ever since announcing our third pregnancy, my husband and I have been enlightened as to the many clever ways friends and strangers have asked the delicate question: "Was this blessed event planned?"

This foray into the ultra-personal comes undoubtedly due to our age (somewhere between legal in all states and in danger of having our licenses revoked due to senility) or to the fact that our two other children are 9 and almost 7.

Another popular follow-up is, "Do you know what it is?" Answering "a baby" is simply not enough for these people. Finding out the gender, however, isn't that easy. Our 20-week ultrasound nearly turned disastrous when the earnest technician explained to my children that the sound waves used on my belly are similar to those used by their Uncle Steve to catch fish. A tense moment ensued, as our son pondered the possibility of Mommy giving birth to a 7-pound walleye.

Silly technology. Instead, I turned to a more reliable source of gender prediction: Wives' Tales.

1. If you crave sweets and fruits, you will have a girl. Result: I'm having a girl.

2. If you crave salty or sour foods, it's a boy. Result: I'm

having a boy. (If you crave everything that's not nailed down, stop it already. It's a baby, not Dumbo.)

3. Lie on your back. If a ring on a thread, held over your belly, moves in circles, it's a boy. Side to side, it's a girl. Result: It's a boy. And could someone please help me up?

4. Low weight gain and healthy good looks mean a boy. Result: Girl. Ack.

5. If chest development is very dramatic, it's a girl. Definitely a Girl. Ack!

6. If your figure in back hasn't changed, it's a boy. Result: Definitely a boy.

7. If the baby's heart rate is slow, it's a boy; if it's fast, you're having a girl. Result: Boy. Turns out that frenzied heart pounding was mine—after stepping on the doctor's scale.

8. Consult a Chinese lunar calendar. This chart, which traces its origins to an ancient royal tomb near Beijing, is based on the month of conception and the mother's age. Result: Girl. And if it's not, tough luck cookie. The vendor at that tomb concession retired three thousand years ago.

So, there you have it. I'm having a boy. Or a girl. And, frankly, I'm relieved. I've seen those walleye come out of the water and, frankly, I'm not sure even a mother could love that face.

24 My Mother Falls in Love – Again

Phil nearly missed Thanksgiving dinner the year my mother fought back into life and began dating again. He called from Atlanta as the stuffing was getting cold on my south Minneapolis dining room table, sheepishly explaining that he had somehow walked down the wrong jetway and onto the wrong plane.

"Don't wait for me," he insisted. "I'll be there for pie."

Judging from the eye-rolling and unfortunate turkey jokes, I suspected that Phil was short for my mother's world. I was right. Too bad. I liked Phil. He bought sweet books for my kids and spoke to me in atrocious French. And he was crazy about my mother, helping her—helping all of us—consider a scenario that seemed both impossible and inevitable: Love. Again.

Phil wasn't the first or last man my mother would date after my father died. But it took her years to even consider the possibility. The first year after his death was hell, the second year was worse. That was when her friends fell away, eager to get back to their own lives. When expectations were high that my mother would be done with grief.

I would visit her in the lovely townhouse she set up after selling our family home and found that heartache comes in the little things. The single-serving frozen dinners. The security system. The restaurant reservations for five: Two couples, one widow.

I realized that her midnight calls to me weren't the result of confusion over our different time zones. It was then that she felt most alone in the world. She told me that one night, while driving her car down the freeway, she began to wonder why she shouldn't just drive off the bridge. But then she thought of us, her three kids, all grown up but still in need of a mother.

And so, when she began to talk about men who weren't the plumber or landscaper, I felt incredible relief. I shook my head at people my age who would complain to Ann and Abby that their widowed parents were embarrassing them by reaching out for romance anew.

"So," I wanted to say in my best Polish grandmother accent, "you want that she should sit in the dark for the rest of her life?"

The process was amusing, to be sure. Question: Is there anything worse than being 10 years old and realizing that your parents are having sex? Answer: Yes, being 40 and realizing the same thing.

Don't worry, my mother would joke. I won't get pregnant. She'd pull out her favorite joke. Question: What's the most effective birth control method among people over 60? Answer: Nudity.

Then one day, eight years after my father died, I picked up the phone and my mother was giddy. She was getting married. So I dyed my shoes green and stood beside her as she recited vows outside an adobe restaurant in northern New Mexico. I told her, in front of our family and closest friends, how awed I was at her bravery.

She and Jack merged their art collections and family photos and, in their seven years together, traveled the globe and saw every movie before I did. A few weeks before he died, also of cancer, she startled me as she told me across her breakfast table: "I'll never marry again. I won't do that to you kids."

"Mom," I said, "you're only 70. You can't possibly . . . Of course we'd support. . . "

Then the truth spilled from her.

"I can't do this again," she said. This excruciating loss of love. Twice in one life is enough.

After Jack died, she got their house in order and flew alone to Florida. Ever the organizer, she sent each of her children her full itinerary, a visit to cousins here, my father's best friend from childhood there, down the coast to Hollywood, Key Largo, Key West.

I wondered whether she thought we just wouldn't notice the large gaps of time when she would be alone, visiting no one, driving a rented Cadillac along highways she'd never traveled.

I envisioned alligators and lecherous men, flat tires and dead cell phone batteries. But, hey, she didn't ask my permission. She needed to feel free, unencumbered. She needed to escape people, condolence cards and the house.

And I needed to let her.

25 Sex—We'll Get Around to It

On a plane recently, I picked up a woman's magazine and tore into an article about the sexual challenges faced by parents of young children. With kids 8 and 6, I was eager to find out how we fared as a couple on this delicate matter, and whether everybody else was also lying about what they're doing behind closed doors.

According to the article, my husband and I are in big trouble. Apparently, we're supposed to be in the same room at the same time.

When we do end up in bed at the same time, we are rarely alone. Chances are good that if that man O mine reaches over and touches something soft, it'll be Peanut, the Beanie Baby. And when he whispers, "Take 'em off," I respond immediately. The wool socks are off. But everything else stays on in this Godforsaken Minnesota Siberia.

Apparently, the authors also think a nice piece of lingerie would help. The problem is, I haven't seen a new Victoria's Secret catalog in...10 minutes. And I'll tell you her secret: That girl hasn't eaten in three weeks. I'd look equally trim in a red silk Miracle Bra if I'd consider skipping dinner once in a while. Talk about a miracle.

So, forget lingerie. How about a "guest appearance" in the shower? Get over it! We have a clawfoot tub. Any attempt at a coy entrance would likely result in seriously bodily harm to him, me, or Rubber Duckie.

Okay, maybe they're right. Maybe we are in a rut, always having sex at the same time. (What can we do? Our anniversary falls on the same date every year...); same position (awake, usually); same pacing (between the time the 6-year-old needs to go to the bathroom and the 8-year-old starts sleepwalking – a good two minutes). At least we're trying.

To prove it, we accept the author's challenge to "let our fantasies energize and inspire us to be adventurous." We are lying in bed in the middle of the day. Both kids are away on play dates, where they'll be for at least one more hour. Even the laundry baskets are empty. There is only one glorious thing for us to do.

Take a nap.

Sex? Sure, we'll get around to it. When the kids are in college.

26 Feeling Lucky

We were dining recently at the kids' favorite restaurant (hint: over 1 billion sold, half a billion successfully digested) when a boy of about 10 approached our table.

"Can I have those?" he asked politely. It wasn't our French fries he wanted, thank God. It was the Monopoly game-board stickers we'd been given along with our order. All he had to do, he said, was collect enough stickers to create one Monopoly and he'd be rich. What struck me most as I reflected later on the request was how sweet the scenario seemed. He didn't just *think* he would win. He knew it.

I remember that feeling very well.

I was about his age when a radio station launched a gimmicky promotion called "Think Mink." All I had to do was answer the telephone with "Think Mink!" every time it rang, and when the deejay called my house, I'd be the proud owner of a mink coat. Political correctness aside, I have no idea what a 9-year-old in Albuquerque, New Mexico, would do with mink skins hanging down to her ankles. It didn't matter. What mattered was that I was going to win. I knew it.

So when did it end? When did I lose that precious child-like belief that something wonderful would happen just because I willed it to? When did I begin to inspect the slope of the softball toss at the State Fair before giving my kids a quarter? When did I stop believing I could win the cake walk?

When did I become such a cynic?

I suppose it comes with the territory called adult life. Too many disappointments. Too many stories about doctored apple juice and other improprieties on the front page of the newspaper. Just work hard, I tell myself, and hope for the best.

Then my daughter, Sydney, announced she'd like a watch for her eighth birthday. And the cynical me thawed as another childhood memory flashed into my head. I was walking into a hardware store with my dad on a sunny Saturday morning. We held hands, and the joy I felt at getting him all to myself was indescribable. Hanging down from the ceiling were huge numbers; match those numbers to those on circulars handed out at the store entrance and you'd win a prize. I didn't have to look at my circular. I knew I had won. Sure enough, I walked out of the store with a spiffy new watch.

So maybe I haven't really stopped believing I'm lucky. I've just redefined what lucky means. The watch is long gone, and even now, living in Minnesota, I have no desire for a mink coat. But there's no one luckier than a woman who, many years after her father has passed away, still feels the warmth and depth of his love.

27 I'm Home Alone!

Hubby and the kids extended their stay down south for a few days last month and I found myself Home Alone. Well, technically, I wasn't alone since the baby came back with me. But the way I figure it, you're on your own until the day your progeny shouts from the high chair: "Mom, is that Chunky Monkey ice cream on your diet?" So, as I was saying, I found myself home alone.

And I did what any self-respecting woman would do when a world of possibilities suddenly, gloriously, opens up to her. I went to the grocery story. Wait! It gets better! I went a little crazy there.

I skipped giddily down aisle after aisle, flinging foods into my cart that I never knew existed. Scones with currants!!! What are currants? Who cares? I want them! I wept in the dairy aisle, reaching for a name-brand Gouda that wasn't, and never would be, on Temporary Price Reduction. I rejoiced in the bread aisle, knowing that for two self-indulgent days I could have a dark, low-fat, high-fiber fling without hearing a single child groaning "yechhhh!"

I came home laughing. Ha, ha, ha! But more decadent surprises awaited me. I wanted a drink of water. And as I reached into the cabinet, I realized that I didn't have to drink out of the green cup. I could have light blue. Or dark blue.

Or white! Wait...I had enough hours left to drink out of every single one of them! And look! There's the dishwasher! It's almost too daring to admit this, but I ran it and it wasn't even full.

But that is not all. Oh, no, that is not all. I took a shower until there was no more hot water left. I didn't floss my teeth. I stayed up until 2 a.m. reading a novel. The next morning, I wandered down to the bakery and bought the largest cup of coffee they had. Then I had another. I ate chocolate bread for breakfast, read another novel with the time I saved not packing lunches, skipped lunch (boring meal) and ate cereal for dinner. Reeses Puffs. Two bowls. Hey, I need the calcium; I'm nursing.

But, alas, I was running out of time. The plane was landing at 9 p.m. So I unloaded the dishwasher to destroy the evidence. Then I grabbed the baby and sat down. I held her and listened to the sweet, simple sound of her breathing. Just the two of us. For one peaceful, uninterrupted hour. Then we headed to the airport.

Of course I was happy to see them. And when they asked me if I had been lonely, I said, "Well, a little." So please, let's keep the details of my wild adventure to ourselves. After all, if my husband ever delights me with currant scones, I'd never want him to know he wasn't the first.

28 Lice Lesson

Well, the kids begged and begged for a pet, so we finally broke down. Some people would say that lice should not be put in the same category as, say, a dog or cat, or even ferret. I disagree. We've had our lice for months now, and I'm proud to say that our new little friends have added immeasurable texture to our lives.

1. They have taught us a new way to communicate. We scratch.

2. They've brought our family closer together. We've canceled birthday parties, sleep-overs, even school, to be together. What family needs outside activities when you can stay home and gather 'round the stove to sterilize combs?

3. They've taught us the courage to speak the truth. We are now able to verbalize bold phrases such as, "You know that winter cap your kid borrowed from us? Really bad idea." And also, "We are good people. Really we are."

4. Our lice have instilled in us the patience of Job. I mean, what is time, really? We now have experienced the Zen-like freedom of sitting for hours (and I mean hours) running our fingers through one another's hair. So what if it's with a nit comb?

5. We have broadened our world to include exciting new places. One of them is the Laundromat on our corner.

6. We have learned how much stuff we can live without. The kids no longer even notice how many of their stuffed animals are living a life of seclusion, safely bagged in the basement. Less is more!

7. We have become a family of poets. Here's mine:

    Some day we will fix
    Your hair with Nix
    And when we do,
    I'll buy a Twix.

(You should hear my Haiku!)

8. We have saved a lot of money on haircuts. No one will cut our hair anymore.

9. We have learned the true meaning of friendship and who our real friends are. We don't have any real friends.

10. We are so preoccupied and exhausted, the kids don't even ask for a dog anymore.

   But the very, very best thing about lice? They are incredibly loyal. Cats stray, dogs run away. But lice…they never—ever—leave you.

29 Jealous of the GPS

I've heard it said that there are two types of people who are incapable of taking a driving trip together without at least one day of window-rattling fighting. These two types would be any man and any woman who happen to be married to each other. Even with good intentions and a giddy sense of reclaimed youth as they take to the road (best experienced if they ignore large children with iPods in the back seat), it is an inescapable reality of marital travel. Within hours, she will tell him he is going the wrong way. He will suggest that, perhaps, she is reading the map upside down. Then the burst of angry words, followed by silence, then laughter at the silliness of such behavior when, for goodness sakes, we are on vacation!, ultimately crescendoing in a powerful, primal urge to repeat the adventure soon, despite the pain. Much like childbirth.

So when planning to rent a car to drive across France, from highway interchanges in Paris at speeds of 140 kilometers per hour to cobblestone roads in Medieval villages, we did stop for a moment and wonder if we might schedule couples' oral surgery instead. Glad we didn't, though. Because this time, we had a secret. We had Marguerite.

Marguerite was the sultry voice of our car's Global Positioning System. And the minute she first spoke, I knew that this would be a road trip like none other.

Driving trips have been a staple of our lives since way before children. The California coast, Florida Keys, Beartooth Pass, the Black Hills, New Mexico, Nebraska Furniture Mart (hey, it was on the way). We have long valued driving for its flexibility and its views, its false sense of being in control and its handy solution to avoiding five airline tickets. Looking back with the maturity of age, I might conclude that any tension experienced along the way could be due, in part, to a slight difference in our planning styles.

Mine looks something like this: "Go to France. Rent car. Find nearest youth hostel."

Husband's approach:

```
Day One: PARIS TO LOIRE VALLEY. Hertz Car Rental at
CDG Conf. No. C9600391190 11:30 am pick up PEUGEOT
407 Satellite Navigation Intermediate Special
Manual Air. Unlimited mileage, charge to Chase MC,
take personal liability, don't take CDW Hertz NO.
52247, CDP NO. 205285 TOTAL CHARGES BEFORE PERSONAL
LIABILITY 357.60 EURO.
```

Over the years, we have worked diligently to appreciate one another's approaches without going so far as to embrace it as our own.

Him to me: "Irresponsible!"

Me to him: "Anal!"

He has experienced the marvel of serendipitous encounters off the beaten path; getting lost has led us to kind souls who become lifelong friends or, sometimes, to a view so beautiful it nearly stops our hearts.

I have grown to cherish the sweet sound of hotel clerks saying, "Oh, yes, we were expecting you."

But a human being can flex only so far. This is why we welcomed Marguerite as though she were a rich, old aunt.

Marguerite joined our family in Paris, with her convincing British accent, confident grasp of geography and patient-yet-firm commands - an unbeatable combination of Mary Poppins and Ask Jeeves. Our 13-year-old son, who fortunately inherited his father's skill at programming stuff with buttons, eagerly ordered our route: First, the spectacular Loire Valley and its majestic chateaux, then down to Biarritz on the southwestern coast, across the Midi to Carcassonne and on to Provence.

Marguerite, so named by a contest held in the back seat, wasn't ruffled by any of it. "Please turn right in 200 mee-tahs," she would say from behind the dashboard.

"Prepare to turn left in 500 mee-tahs," and, finally, "Now, turn left."

My husband, who was never too bullish on my mapping skills, obeyed Marguerite of the sultry voice with equal parts schoolboy and lap dog. If, by chance, he would zig when he should have zagged, kindly Marguerite would get him back on track pronto.

"Please make a U-turn, if possible."

And, of course, he would. "She's firm but fair," he said at one point to no one in particular. "Infinitely patient. Forgiving."

The kids must have noticed my growing concern at being bested by a chick in a box.

"You have one thing over Marguerite," my 16-year-old

daughter piped up in a tremendous show of comfort. "A uterus."

The 7-year-old, who didn't like Mommy insisting that she hold my hand or please get that Vittel water bottle cap out of her mouth, was less generous.

"Marguerite takes care of us," she said. "She isn't strict, like SOME people."

Or when really peeved at me, a sing-songy, "Daddy has a girlfriend, Daddy has a ..."

Secretly, though, I was more in love with Marguerite than anyone else was. For the first time in memory, I relaxed and gazed out the window as we cruised past idyllic farmhouses and castles, onto narrow bridges and broad, billboard-free highways for an entire week, laughing all the way.

We bid adieu to Marguerite in Cannes—a melancholy moment, to be sure. Mostly because we learned that the Hertz rental car office was closed for lunch (this was France, after all). So we paced and fretted about extra fees and missing our connection and hungry kids and the heat and why didn't we plan better and, for heaven's sake we're in Cannes! And, well.

And, well, my family was back. Noisy, fussy, funny, human. We vowed to carry on as best we could. Marguerite would expect no less.

30 Fruit Basket

S he leaned over the kitchen table, meticulously crafting tiny pieces of fruit from Sculpey clay and toothpicks. First a bunch of grapes, then an apple and a pear. The basket was her *chef d'oeuvre*—a square of delicate ivory topped with a brown handle and wrapped in brown weaving. When it was complete, she held it delicately in her 8-year-old hands. To me, it was the most beautiful thing in the world.

We carefully placed the fruit basket with a dozen other clay pieces, among them a tiny bride holding a bouquet of flowers, into a shoe box, and drove to an art gallery near our house. The gallery owner had, a week earlier, invited my daughter Sydney to sell her work in a month-long children's art exhibit, and she was giddy with excitement.

Despite the stifling summer heat, we had spent the weekend with our oven turned high to harden her creations, then sat at the table with a black marker and masking tape, thoughtfully pricing each piece. The night of the opening, she wore her best dress and a decorative headband. And she stood stoically as a crowd of spectators walked by her, politely pausing before choosing to buy some other child's beaded earrings, some other child's pencil sketch of a bear, some other child's clay figurines.

The gallery owner, an artist herself, would not allow her

young protégé to feel discouraged. "Return at the end of the month," she instructed confidently, to be paid for the many pieces Sydney was sure to sell by then. Sydney smiled sweetly but, as the month progressed, I noticed that she didn't touch her clay at home.

Many times I drove by the gallery and came close to going in, not to check on Sydney's art, but to secretly buy it. I thought about asking friends to do the same. Then the rational side of me reared its annoying head, reminding me that we can't possibly shield our children entirely from the inevitable disappointments in life. But we can give them the tools to deal with those disappointments with grace, humor and perspective.

So my husband, who left corporate life to create musical children's videos he hopes someone will buy, and I, who write articles I hope someone will read, talked to our daughter about the sticky business of defining "art." About how strange it is that what one person loves another detests. About how brave artists are to share the most personal pieces of themselves with the world, particularly when they're only 8.

At the end of the month, we picked up all but one of Sydney's creations. Her tiny clay bride did sell—to the gallery owner—who keeps it up front for all to see. And the most beautiful clay fruit basket in the world sits just where it should, on the window sill in my kitchen, as a daily reminder of the sweet, fragile journey called growing up.

31 A not-so-merry Go Round

We lifted off on the Sky Glider with an energizing jolt, carried thirty feet into the air to enjoy a bird's-eye view of the charming Santa Cruz beach boardwalk. It was a glorious June afternoon, the fifth day of a nearly flawless family vacation to California. The largest and liveliest seaside amusement park on the West Coast was below our sandy feet to the right, the Pacific Ocean crashed into the shore at our left. Memories flooded back, so rich, so clear, so . . . horrifying.

Oh my God! I hate these things!

But it was too late. We were moving, latched lamely into a little blue chair with an opening the size of Texas between the seat and the guard rail—perfect for the 4-year-old sitting next to me to slip through and fall . . . down . . . down . . . down . . . is that cement?

Oh my God!

My sweet child, fortunately, was unaware that we were about to die. She wanted to wave to her father.

"No!" The word escaped my throat like a crow's caw. I wished I were a braver person. I wished I were medicated. With great effort, I changed my tone. "Hold on to the bar with both hands, sweetie pie. Whee!"

She laughed, scooting forward, kicking her feet, lifting

one hand off the bar. I screamed, but in a controlled sort of way.

"Both hands on the bar, love! Keep both hands on the bar!"

I wrenched one of my own hands free and wrapped it around her tiny waist. I pulled her toward the seat back, clutching her tightly, trying not to strangle her.

"Let's move back a little bit, sweetheart. Then you can see more."

My mind was spinning with questions: How many hours had we been on this horrid thing? Why were other riders smiling? Is that rust on the cable?

Down below, Daddy had pulled out his camera, obviously unaware that this would be the last picture he ever captured of his wife and youngest child. Why was he smiling?

Then he turned. Where was he going? Oh my God! He and the two big kids were heading to the ride's exit. We were going to live! Everyone! We're going to live!

After what seemed like three days, a painfully bored teenage attendant unlatched us and we hopped out.

"How was it?" hubby asked.

"Great!" we both yelled.

Later, I came across a blurb about the Sky Glider in a neat little guidebook called *Around San Francisco with Kids*: "The overhead chair lift travels high over the park," it said, "so be careful. The height could scare young kids."

32 Getting a Dog: How Hard Could It Be?

When I was a kid, our family got a dog the way most families did. First, my two brothers and I killed the goldfish, lost the guinea pig, and watched the hamster eat her young as we sat at the kitchen table nibbling on Pop-Tarts. We were ready for a new pet experience.

So we begged. Our parents said, "Over our dead bodies." We wore them down. And eventually Charlie, rejected by his previous owner, arrived, eagerly welcomed by three grateful children who promised to walk him every day— unless we didn't feel like it.

A 3-year-old dachshund of questionable breeding and plentiful warts, Charlie was destined to live a life of table scraps, periodic scratches behind the ears, and romps in our sunny backyard, chasing squirrels and barking at the mailman.

I loved Charlie with a passion reserved for little girls sandwiched between two brothers who did not care to understand the complexities of her psyche. And I refused to accept that Charlie was anything but Best in Show. My parents didn't flinch when, at age 8, I entered him in a community-wide dog show. I walked him in the grand circle (he stalled, then sat). I lifted him onto the table for the judge to examine his teeth (a lovely shade of amber). He growled at the judge, then bit him. The understanding man, perhaps a father himself, bestowed upon Charlie and me a magnificent third-place ribbon, white and silky. I cherished that ribbon until my older brother felt the need to clarify that there were only three dogs in the competition.

That brother is a lawyer now.

Charlie died seven years later, much the way he had lived: quietly, with a little heave and a hack and a final breath. I sobbed as we buried him in the backyard and my younger brother asked: "Next time, can we get a real dog?"

Now, almost forty years later, I'm standing at the PetSmart in Minneapolis with a decorative blue leash wrapped around my ankles. My 6-year-old is shouting at me to not put my boot down on the three-pound dog who is now running my life.

Pepe and his heftier four-pound cousin, Chica, are enrolled in a puppy class, but I am quickly realizing that they are not the students. Eileen, the instructor who can make dogs sew quilts by simply staring in their direction, seems skeptical of my abilities.

"They're barking incessantly?" she asks me. "What are you doing about that?"

I worry that if I tell Eileen the truth—that I'm getting down on my hands and knees and whispering "sshhhhhhhh" to dogs who jump up and lick my face before barking louder —she'll flunk me.

"I put them in their kennel!" I tell her.

"Yes, that's right," Eileen responds happily. "You have to remember who's in charge."

Yes. Well.

Everything felt so familiar at first. The kids killed the goldfish and gave away the gerbils. We offered them a guinea pig. They begged for a dog. We said, "Over our dead bodies." They wore us down.

Then. To my surprise, there were no Charlies anymore. In 2004, there were "breeds" and "breeders." And Web sites. And societies and magazines and doggie treats shaped like truffles. And schnoodles and labradoodles getting massages and acupuncture.

Friends directed us to an online "breed selector": Did we want a large dog? A medium-sized dog? A toy? How would we rate and prioritize 674 essential traits of dog ownership? We hit "submit" and eagerly counted the seconds until our perfect dog would be revealed.

My children reeled in horror at the result: "A pug?" shouted my 13-year-old son. "It looks like it ran into a snowplow!"

The 6-year-old was kinder. "I like the way they taped on the tail."

I tried the emotional appeal: "Kids," I asked, "doesn't every dog deserve a good home? Besides, pugs were the dogs of Chinese royalty! Wow!"

Silence.

Their father took a different approach: "The pug or nothing."

We found two pugs from a highly recommended breeder: A male who needed a $900 hip surgery and a female we could have for a steal—$1,100—if we'd bring her back twice for breeding. To Milwaukee.

"OK, how about a dachshund? Charlie was a dachshund."

I dashed off a brief and cheery e-mail to one of the best breeders in the Upper Midwest:

Dear Ms. Dachshund Breeder:

We'd be delighted to purchase one of your dogs. We have three school-aged children. My husband and I both had dachshunds growing up. Mine was an award-winner. (So sue me.)

Ms. Dachshund Breeder wrote back quickly. I was doomed. How many hours a week would the dog be home alone? Did we have a fence? (Uh-oh.) How young was our youngest child? Her dogs didn't like too much youthful exuberance. . .

I refused to give up.

Dear Ms. Dachshund Breeder:

Thank you for your prompt reply. We do not have a fence, but we are eagerly planning to build one because my husband and I have little else to do, and there's money sitting in our children's college funds that we'd rather spend on wooden posts. Enclosed, please find my children's most recent test scores, references from several heads of state, and a freshly baked apple pie.

Would you believe that I never heard from Ms. Dachshund Breeder again? Well! Who cares about stupid wiener dogs?! We'd go to the pound. We'd save a life! We'd have a dog this very afternoon!

But the pound was moving to a bigger site and all they had was one 86-pound labrador whose eye-level gaze with our 6-year-old did not inspire her to think "play date." The pound people directed us to a world called "animal rescue." But the animal rescue people referred us to an online application requiring *three* references before they would schedule a site visit to see our fence and, quite likely, check *our* teeth. Rescue puppies aren't eager to get rescued by just anyone, apparently. Maybe we'd have a fourth child.

My 15-year-old daughter threw up her arms. "We're NEVER getting a dog! I'll take the guinea pig!"

Then, just when all hope seemed lost, she spotted a small ad in the newspaper for something called a papillon - French for butterfly, which is the shape of the creature's ears but also short for "I'm French, you're not, I'll poop wherever I want." Papillons are small (6 to 8 pounds), smart, friendly and they adore children. And best of all, a breeder was willing to sell us one without running a perp check first.

On a Sunday morning in June, hubby and the kids drove two hours to meet the breeder halfway. They met and fell in love in a Wal-Mart parking lot.

The kids, that is, and two perky papillon pups: a 3.8-pound black male and a 4.2-pound red female. They bought them both.

Who cares? At last, our family had what we hoped for: Eight pounds of dog.

We did put up that fence. And trainer Eileen still has hope for me. We buy organic dog food and never feed them table scraps. We reward good behavior with treats shaped like truffles. We wash them with lovely scented dog shampoo that's nicer than the stuff I buy for myself. We brush their teeth and clip their nails and never, ever say no to them because Eileen says we can't.

Periodically, we take them to the Hundred Dollar Store, a.k.a. the vet. But sometimes late at night, when everyone is asleep and I sit writing at my computer, Chica and Pepe lie next to me on a blanket in a plain grocery box, occasionally licking my hand. Then, nose to nose, they fall asleep, breathing softly. And I know they're not dreaming about Pup-Peroni treats or doggie acupuncture. I'll bet they're dreaming about chasing squirrels under a hot sun in our fenced backyard, where they feel safe and loved.

Just like Charlie.

33 DEAR GOD, A Family Cookbook

About fifteen years into my married life, the cookbooks stopped arriving. That was when my mother-in-law finally accepted that her son really did commit to a woman who considered Reese's Puffs cereal a surprisingly satisfying dinner alternative. I'm not a bad cook, actually. It's just that I follow the State Fair theory of culinary arts: Make it big, fanciful, and once a year.

Still, until recently I secretly fretted that the phenomenal cooks and bakers on my husband's side of the family (every darn woman *in* his family, actually) were disappointed that I was not cooperating by passing down my share of cherished recipes made with love for generations by *my* ancestors.

My husband's grandmother was born in St. Louis in 1906. She married at 16, lived to 94, ran a family farm and small dry goods store, and skimmed fresh cream from the cows' milk for her husband's breakfast cereal every morning. That's why he only lived to 100. She experimented with dishes that have become family legacies: sweet and sour meatballs, baked fish with sour cream sauce, baked chicken with noodles, peas and onions, spaghetti casserole, and her famous graham cracker cake with a coup de grace of chocolate mocha frosting. No family event is complete without at least two of them.

Food was more than nourishment for her four children

and, later, twenty-six grandchildren (including spouses) and thirty-three great-grandchildren. It was the magnet that pulled everyone to her big wooden kitchen table in south Texas to talk and laugh and fight and act like a family. Her daughter, my mother-in-law, delights in trying new recipes. She arrived in Minneapolis from Texas recently with an ice chest full of meat (fajitas, corned beef, short ribs) despite our insistence that one could, in fact, find a grocery store north of Kansas City. Her sweets are divine, particularly her kuchen, a light and sweet pastry rolled out long, then baked and cut into small pieces.

My sisters-in-law were all up to the challenge she presented. Jolene is a registered dietitian who studied cooking in Europe and lived for years in San Francisco, where she became expert at Asian and French cuisine. More than a thousand cookbooks line the shelves of her spacious sitting room.

Carol's kids, now grown, beg for her carrot cake whenever they're home for a visit. Peggy makes tofu irresistible and bakes fresh challah every Friday night for her kosher Jewish home.

And then there's me. There's no political agenda lurking behind my reluctance to experiment in the kitchen. It's just that, from the moment we started dating, hubby started cooking. I think he sensed it would be a good idea.

But that legacy thing kept gnawing at me. If I couldn't offer up comfort foods like tender brisket, spaghetti casserole, corned beef and cabbage or graham cracker cake, what could I contribute? Then it came to me...

My 14-year-old daughter, Sydney, stands at our long kitchen counter with her paternal grandmother. Their hands are now the same size and they move in one effortless motion.

Together, they have kneaded bread and sliced apples for pie. But tonight it's kuchen, my daughter's favorite. Grandmother gently takes granddaughter through the steps, sifting flour, baking powder and sugar, then smoothing in the butter, egg yolks and vanilla. They spread on plum jam, sprinkle the dough with cinnamon sugar and chopped nuts, then roll it up jelly-roll fashion. Once it's baked, they'll cut it into strips and serve it warm.

I'll be waiting, proud and relieved, with a big cup of milk.

THE RECIPE: KUCHEN

Makes about 8 dozen pieces. (Best results if made with one's grandchild.)

4 c. flour	3 eggs, separated
2 t. baking powder	1 t. vanilla
1 c. sugar	1 16-oz. jar plum jam
½ lb. (2 sticks) butter	1 c. cinnamon sugar
1 c. sour cream	1 ½ c. pecans, chopped
½ tsp. baking soda	1 egg white, lightly beaten

Sift together flour, baking powder and sugar. Work in butter with a pastry cutter or two knives, as you would a pie crust. Mix sour cream and baking soda and add to flour mixture. Add egg yolks and vanilla. Form into smooth dough, divide into 8 parts, cover with plastic wrap and freeze for several hours.

Defrost dough. Preheat oven to 350°. On a well-floured board, roll out each dough part to a rectangle about ¼-inch thick. Spread with plum jam and sprinkle with cinnamon sugar and chopped nuts. Roll up jelly-roll fashion, starting with a long side of the rectangle. Brush with lightly beaten egg white and sprinkle with cinnamon and sugar and chopped pecans.

Before baking, to keep size and shape of rolls uniform, cut pieces of foil 6" x 12" and fold up sides so that bottom of foil tray is about 4" across. Spray with Pam and put each roll into foil tray. Bake 20 minutes at 350°. When cool, wrap the rolls in foil to freeze. Kuchen must be frozen before cutting. When ready to use, remove from freezer, heat 15 minutes in a 350° oven and cut into slices.

To freeze finished kuchen: Before cutting, wrap the baked, cooled kuchen tightly and freeze. When ready to use, remove from freezer, heat for about 15 minutes in a 350° oven and cut into slices.

From *La Pinata Cookbook* published by the Junior Service League of McAllen, Texas.

34 Remembering Young Love

S he walks down the stairs in a lacy white sundress. She's as big as a minute and as young as an almost-bride can be, still wearing her retainer. I've adored her since she was a child, a flower girl in our wedding. For years she wanted to be a writer, sending me her increasingly sophisticated school reports. I saved every one in a folder. (Then she got smart and applied to medical school.) Still, I watch her development with the special sweetness reserved for aunts like me. Soon she'll dress in white again to become a married woman.

Today we've driven in the rain to her bridal shower. As I watch her graciously open gifts, including my sleek Gibson pitcher from Crate & Barrel, I'm suddenly struck by the vast emotional space between us—between what we know. I inhabited her world once, in which the future was all about playing house and candlelit dinners. I can't remember when, exactly, I veered off that highway down a somewhat bumpier road, but I'm guessing I did it about the time Cathi Hanauer did.

Hanauer is the author of the best-seller, *The Bitch in the House*. I read it cover-to-cover on the plane on my way here. It would trigger as much familiarity in my sweet niece as a snowstorm in Buenos Aires. Hanauer's book is a hold-onto-your-hat collection of essays by women writers, many of them of a certain age (mine), and most of them familiar with piles of dirty underwear. None of them has much trouble being candid about love and sex, marriage and motherhood, anger and acceptance.

The book is hardly an anti-male diatribe. If anything, it's a 300-page affirmation that neither gender has cornered the market on confusion when it comes to human relationships.

Feminist Natalie Angier, for example, leaps out of the starting gate with a diatribe against President Bush, but ends with a personal truth about what carrying the torch has amounted to: loneliness.

Writer Hannah Pine attempts to explain why she and her husband have chosen an open marriage. Instead of titillation and temptation, though, one is left feeling that these two are nothing if not misled.

There are essays about a first marriage at 46, about how easily couples can become strangers, about how we vow to approach relationships differently from our parents, but seldom do.

Perhaps the book's most powerful moment comes from Elissa Schappell, who shares the horrible moment she unleashed her anger on her two young children.

Hanauer (whose husband, Daniel Jones, edited the appropriately titled *Bastard on the Couch*) conceived of the book several years ago when she couldn't figure out why her "perfect" life was so hard. She had a loving husband, two sweet kids, professional success and yet . . .

"I found myself overwhelmed by the juggling act," she says. "It was chaotic, not the way I felt it should be." She began e-mailing friends and found that many of them, too, felt stressed out, angry. Division of roles, struggles with monogamy, with finding time to think, led her and Jones, more than once, to "fling around the `d` word."

In a country whose leaders are pushing for the "m" word—marriage—it might be helpful if they also offered an addendum to those marriage vows: Advice on what to do when a young bride or groom, filled with desperation at how hard it can be to live with another human being, wants to heave that Gibson pitcher across the room.

But on this gently raining day, I want nothing but my niece's happiness. I smile as she and her handsome fiancé open their Cuisinart, Calphalon, Corningware. Someday she, too, will inhabit my world, where people know more than they might wish about hurt and selfishness, disappointment and boredom. But I'm hoping that by that time, she'll also have found out some things about forgiveness and lasting love, and about just how sexy it can feel when someone knows everything about you and loves you anyway.

Now isn't the time to tell her these things. So I'll pack the book away and pull it out in a decade or so when she just might need it. "Marriage is not idyllic all the time," Hanauer says. "But surviving the hard times makes it more meaningful."

I don't wish my niece hard times. They'll come anyway. And when they do, I know she'll draw on the inner strength she's always carried to ride out the storms.

35 White Dress, Worn Only Once

I saw it in a magazine and that was that. I had found my wedding dress. It was hardly couture (less Vera Wang, more Very Plain), but it was lovely and feminine and my father told us to be good to each other as he lifted my veil. And of course, that was our intention.

My intention, two decades and one split later, was to clean up after myself—another bit of advice my father would have wholeheartedly supported. So, after a speedy 18 months of procrastinating, I plunged into a reconnaissance mission in my former garage and basement, digging through box after box marked "GAIL/SAVE!"

Boxes stuffed with letters from people I love and people I no longer remember, my first newspaper articles (the journalistic term for them is "dreck"). Baby books, yearbooks, riveting day planners (pick up dry cleaning!), teaching notes, photos. So many pieces of my past I was certain I'd want to have and to hold forever. Nah. Into the recycling bin it went.

Then there was that other box. It was long and narrow and it is, to this day, unopened, because, frankly, I can't decide what to do with it. It houses that simple white wedding dress, the one I would someday pass down to the daughter I hoped to have. Divorce was really not in my plans.

I have two lovely daughters now, and my thoughts regarding the fate of that single wedding dress change almost hourly.

I could sell it on eBay. But then I remember I have no idea how to sell anything on eBay.

I could save it for Halloween and go as "Bride of Frankenstein."

But what if someone said: "Wow! Scary! Where did you find that?"

No, I would donate it to "Brides Against Breast Cancer" (bridesagainstbreastcancer.org), where proceeds from wedding dresses grant wishes to terminally ill women. I was very excited about this option until I searched their site and realized that they didn't want my lovely wedding dress. Too old.

Value Village, Goodwill, or some other nonprofit might want it. But, OK, this is stupid. I guess I'd want to know who bought it. Maybe she'd let me buy her a cup of coffee and I could tell her, talking loudly and using my typical big hand gestures, about the happy times and why you carry those moments with you. I might even get a chance to explain how any experience helps us to evolve into more decent human beings before she called the police.

Twincitiesfreemarket.org doesn't seem to want clothes of any kind, but they do have three wallets, two Christmas trees and one box of Styrofoam peanuts, in case you're interested.

Another option keeps gnawing at me. I could hang on to it. Maybe one of my girls, still young but already wiser than I ever was at her age, will someday open that box and see in it the hope and promise with which I wore it, embraced lovingly by her father. Maybe she'll see beginnings, not endings. Maybe she'll wear it without a moment's hesitation. Or maybe she'll decide—and this would be fine with me—to take some delicate piece of it, a swatch of lace, a ribbon or piece of beadwork, and sew it onto a different dress more to her liking. Something old to take into a new life that she would craft.

Yes. For now, at least, I think this is the best solution.

I do. I really do.

36 More Like Jacob

The birthday boy flew around the skating rink on Rollerblades, not slowed down in the least by the nauseating psychedelic lighting or the two pieces of greasy cheese pizza in his stomach. His buddies caught up to him on occasion, and around and around they'd go.

All except for Jacob.

Jacob had come to my son's eighth birthday party on what we quickly realized were false pretenses. Jacob said he could rollerskate. Jacob cannot rollerskate. We rented him rollerskates anyway—the old-fashioned kind with four fat wheels that most boys wouldn't be caught dead wearing these days—and lifted him off the security of the carpet and onto the slick rink.

Go Jacob! Jacob didn't move. Then he got inspired. He waved his arms furiously and did a moonwalk-on-wheels sort of thing, before crashing to the floor. Several times. It wasn't just amusing to watch this sweet, quiet kid; it was humbling. For the next hour, Jacob ignored the stares and giggles of the hoard of hotshots breezing past to the thumping beat of Britney Spears and the Backstreet Boys, and stayed focused on one goal: Moving forward. He allowed other children to give him an impromptu lesson in staying upright, waved un-self-consciously to his friends as they lapped him again and again, laughed when he fell, clapped every time he inched forward, and made my husband and me stop and think about how seldom we are in the presence of a truly gracious human being.

Particularly one who is only seven.

Jacob reminded me of how hard it usually is to admit that we don't know how to do something. I work on this one with my kids all the time, assuring them that a solid B on a math test is really, really OK; that performing a piano piece in front of a crowd is an amazing feat in and of itself, even if you did land on a sharp instead of a flat. I feel their impatience when I try to tell them something about their computer, their book report, their sometimes rocky alliances with friends. What I usually get is: "Mommmmm! I already KNOW!" I fear they get this tendency from me. I burn things, break things, misuse things, because I'm too old (read: too proud) to ask for help. It's just easier to pretend, I guess.

After watching Jacob, I'm rethinking. Here was a kid who might as well have been wearing a neon sign around his neck: "Can't skate!" So he unabashedly celebrated his baby steps of progress.

Instead of a long, elaborate list of New ear's resolutions this year, I'm making just one: I want to be more like Jacob.

I want to ask for help more often, without feeling embarrassed. I want to feel happy, instead of envious, for friends who lap me in life. I want to laugh out loud when I fall on my butt. And I want to celebrate my own little victories without inhibitions. Who can say when the next big one will come around?

37 Under the Baker's Hat

He was wearing this goofy baker's hat, oversized like something a caricature of a baker would wear. It had neon yellow and blue stripes and it hung over his balding head like a tilted soufflé.

"I like your hat," I told him, trying to maneuver a hungry 5-year-old through the breakfast line without spilling, dropping, or breaking anything. The poor guy was working his brains out, running in and out of the kitchen with bagels, eggs, Apple Jacks cereal. I guess I just wanted him to know somebody noticed.

He smiled, willing to play along. "My son made it," he told me. "In eighth grade. Back then, all the kids had to take home economics—even the boys. He's been gone about seven years now. Car crash."

We stared at each other awkwardly. Then he turned, yanked a hot silver tray out of its holder to refill it with bagels. Keep moving. Keep moving.

We were attending a family retreat—a chance to get away from routines and reality for a few days. Everyone around me seemed to be shifting effortlessly into leisure mode but I, suddenly, could do no such thing. I looked around the dining room. My 5-year-old had seated herself and was slurping down a bowlful of syrup, happily unencumbered by her distracted mother. The 12-year-old was sitting with his buddies as far away from his parents' table as possible. My 14-year-old daughter was reading. My three kids. The oldest, the youngest, the only boy.

I thought about a woman I once met who had lost two sons to a genetic disease. What surprised me most wasn't that she was warm and gracious and working every day in a job that genuinely seemed to interest her. It was that she still wore lipstick. Bright red.

I remembered last summer, when a couple we were getting to know stunned us as we walked together in the heat of the State Fair. They apologized for seeming blue, but the birthday of their son who had died in infancy was that very week. I had no idea. My 5-year-old spontaneously grabbed the mother's hand and pulled her up several rickety stairs to the Ferris wheel, where they rode together high above the crowd. One little head of blond hair, one mother in a sun hat fighting to make her way back through the mindless rhythms of ordinary life.

Bagels. Eggs. Cereal.

I hesitated before walking into the large industrial kitchen, where I found him, his thick hands immersed in a heaping vat of tuna and mayo. He told me his name was Paul. His son was driving with a friend on a rural road on a clear, sunny morning. Hit a pothole. His friend flew through the windshield but only got a few scratches. The car rolled twice, into one tree, then another. His son was rushed to a trauma center where he died the next day. Two weeks after turning 17.

"He was going too fast," Paul said, breaking into a kids-today grin. "Not wearing a seat belt. Otherwise, he would have lived."

More mayo. More seasoning salt.

Paul's other three kids are adults now. He has three grandkids, too, including a 2-year-old granddaughter who lives just up the hill. He's especially sweet on her. Aside from his weekend work serving food at this family retreat center, he and his wife run a video and tanning store in town. They're busy, happy mostly.

Still, "it's hard to lose a child," he says almost apologetically. "The wife's going on faith." But it's been seven years. He's learned that, after a while, nobody asks any more. So he wears the goofy hat. Maybe just to feel covered in a little comfort. Or maybe it's in hope that someone will notice and serve him up a moment to talk about his son.

38 Annual Review

Hiking two miles upward toward Grand Teton two weeks ago, we navigated a narrow, rocky path—two adults, three children, five walking sticks—as the whoosh of snowmelt rushed off toward majestic Jenny Lake. It would be our last summer hurrah, our final smothering clutch before the kids returned to school. Before we returned to work.

Before I returned to obligations I had carefully avoided in my pre-vacation frenzy. September would mean diving headlong into performance reviews, the annual opportunity to encourage my staff to move out of their comfort zones toward greater professional fulfillment. Around here, the task is largely met with the enthusiasm better reserved for swallowing Vaseline.

Nothing should be that tough. Besides, I can tell my staff, I'm the one who should be sweating it out. I face the biggest performance review of all. It started last night at sundown with Rosh Hashanah, the Jewish New Year, and will continue for 10 days until Yom Kippur, the Day of Atonement. In short, I have a little more than a week to search my soul before the figurative Book of Life closes, inscribing my name (I hope) for another year.

Forget missed deadlines or a disorganized staff meeting. How do I rate as a human being?

Each year, I search for answers to this question wherever I can. While on our summer trip, I breezed through a trim little book by Rabbi Harold Kushner called *Living a Life That Matters: Resolving the Conflict Between Conscience and Success.* Kushner, who also wrote the bestseller *When Bad Things Happen to Good People*, and the intriguingly titled *How Good Do We Have to Be?*, assures his readers that sainthood is not the goal. (Lucky thing for a girl named Rosenblum.) Rather, he pushes each of us to become a *mensch*—a good person.

In the Tetons, did I stay on the trails and clean up after myself? At work, did I show up on time and resist the temptation to take home extra Post-it notes? (OK, I'll work on that one.) Did I reach out in my community with no expectation of personal payoff? At home, can my husband and children trust me to do what I said I would?

"What kind of people are we?" Kushner asks. "Are we naturally good and pure until external circumstances compromise our goodness? Or are we naturally weak and deceitful, needing conscience or outside authority to keep us in line?" He believes we are both.

"I see every human being as having good and bad tendencies, impulses to charity and impulses to selfishness, the desire to be truthful and the desire to lie," he writes. "These tendencies are in constant tension within us."

I see signposts of that tension in another place: a little folder I've kept near my bed for years. It's filled with a hodgepodge of items: my chronically overambitious list of annual goals relating to my relationships, my health, my job. Oh, the places I'll go! The books I'll read! There's poetry and a self-portrait by my son, then 7. This year I added a mantra

I've kept in my day planner since my first post-Sept. 11 plane trip: *What would you do if you weren't afraid?*

On those pages in my folder I chronicle my struggles to find more time, to be more patient, to get more sleep, to reach out, to reach in. I've written "weight training" as a goal for about five years now—"written" being the operative word. Really, though, how many saints have buff arms?

This year I found a new source for reflection: a list of questions that management consultants recommend we ask our staffs during job reviews. Not bad for life reviews, either:

What goals would you like to set for yourself this year? What solutions can you offer? What gets in the way of you doing your job the way you'd like to be doing it? What kind of learning would you like to do? What do you need help with? What are you struggling with?

There is one big difference, though, between job reviews and life reviews. In the former, we're instructed to look forward, to avoid belaboring past transgressions and focus instead on building on strengths, setting goals, devising concrete criteria with which to measure progress.

On the Jewish New Year, we're instructed to look backward, to face those we have hurt and make amends.

To repent, according to Jewish teachings, you must do three things: Feel genuine regret, express that regret to the person you've harmed, and never do the harmful action again.

Still, neither process amounts to a trial. It's more like a trail. Sometimes we wander from it accidentally, or sneak off to find a better view, or throw rocks in our path because we no longer believe in ourselves.

We can usually get back on track with encouragement.

"Good people will do good things, lots of them, because they are good people," Kushner writes. "They will do bad things because they are human . . . But we will never stop asking ourselves, `What kind of person do I want to be?'"

So I'll sit down with each member of my staff and offer praise for good work done. Together we'll pinpoint one or two goals. Then, before the next ten days are up, I'll take out a pen and paper, and do the same for myself.

39 Small Kindnesses

I was standing in front of a bakery case recently, deciding whether to go with the high-fat long john or the higher-fat bear claw. Cleverly, I compromised by buying them both, and pretty much everything else left in the case at 1 p.m. Our work team was celebrating two December birthdays, and even in the Season of Excessive Eating, I didn't anticipate leftovers.

Eleven pastries in a box later, the amiable woman behind the counter grabbed a twelfth, something caramel-gooey with chocolate chips.

"This one is for you, no charge," she said, smiling. Then she pointed her finger at me playfully. "Don't share it."

Now, this was hardly a Chicken Soup moment, but more than two weeks later, I find I'm still thinking about it. Either I need a serious intervention for sugar addiction, or I'm hungry in another way: kindness-hungry. I have a hunch you know what I mean.

Piero Ferrucci does. His book crossed my desk not long ago, and I found the title intriguing - "The Power of Kindness: The Unexpected Benefits of Leading a Compassionate Life." But I found his thesis a little sad.

Ferrucci is a psychotherapist who lives near Florence, Italy—which raises the question: Why would anyone who lives near Florence, Italy, need psychotherapy? But I digress. Ferrucci believes that most of us don't just refuse to be kind. We no longer know *how* to be kind. He says our world has become cold, anxious, difficult, frightening. We are, he says, in a state of "global cooling."

I wouldn't go that far. After all, right now we're still feeling the afterglow of the season of goodwill. We've spent the past few weeks—as individuals, families, churches and businesses—performing countless acts of kindness for others. Toy and food drives, hot meals served, festive parties thrown to share good cheer, good fortune, good nog. I love it all.

The problem is, these acts are all so . . . big. Too big to sustain for longer than a few weeks at best. And I think our world, including little ol' me and little ol' you, could use a few more interactions in the gosh-that-was-nice department, no matter how saccharine-sweet that sounds.

So let me be the first to suggest that the coming year become The Year of Thinking Small. We could take Ferrucci as our guide. Each of his eighteen chapters speaks to a different aspect of small but mighty kindnesses. He even reminds us what they look like.

If that seems too ambitious, perhaps, (in the spirit of small thinking) we can each pick one or two to work on this year. Here's the list, with elaboration on a few:

Honesty with ourselves and others. ("Kindness cannot exist," Ferrucci says, "in a world of masks and phantoms.")

Warmth.

Forgiveness.

Touch.

A Sense of Belonging (which includes bringing those who feel less connected into our circles).

Trust. Mindfulness. Empathy. Humility. Patience. Generosity (material and spiritual). Respect. Flexibility. Remembering. (This means taking the trouble "to preserve the most creative and beautiful heritage that our predecessors left us.") Loyalty. Gratitude.

Service. Joy.

That last one's easy. Just offer someone, when she least expects it, something sweet, like a compliment, a smile, or a gooey pastry, and trust that your little kindness will work in big ways.

40 Where Were You When the Bridge Collapsed?

The panicked e-mails and cell phone calls began almost immediately. They came from London and Brainerd, San Diego and Albuquerque, Washington, D.C., and Austin, Texas.

"I just needed to know ..."

"Will relax when I hear from you ..."

"My heart goes out to you ..."

For a technology-free hour I was clueless, baking chicken and mashing potatoes in my kitchen while an international tragedy was playing out three minutes from my workplace. All that ended, of course, when my 9-year-old daughter switched on the computer to play with her Webkinz and we saw the horrific fallen freeway bridge.

We live in a region of nearly 3 million people, in a state of 5 million, in a country of 300 million, in a world of 6.6 billion. That's a lot of people and rivers and bridges and school buses and, sadly, a lot of pain thrust at us on a daily basis. Yet, while we wring our hands at how technology numbs us, isolates us from one another in deference to machines, all it takes is a great big tragedy to remind us that our world is tiny, really.

My mother was certain that one of her grandchildren was on that school bus. My sister-in-law was certain that I was on that bridge. My old friend Jeff wrote: "Please tell me you weren't in the car last night." In the car.

There were light moments, too. A bemused colleague shared that her high school boyfriend checked in to see if she was OK. I got e-mails from two men I dated briefly before they disappeared like rocket flares. ("Yes, I'm fine," I wanted to write. "But you're not!")

My former colleague Dave Nimmer (now professor emeritus in the school of journalism at the University of St. Thomas) isn't surprised that our ever-shrinking planet grows even smaller during times of tragedy. The media in general, but mostly that big flat screen my worried London cousins call the telly, becomes an "electronic campfire," he says. We gather 'round to watch a woman, a rope tied around her waist, plunge underwater toward a car. We see a school bus perched perilously close to the edge, and folks helping to lower victims in stretchers onto safer ground. We see ourselves. We see our loved ones. And, suddenly, we need to make the call.

"Maybe it's just my age," said Nimmer, 67, who has heard from several colleagues and friends over the past few days, "but it reminds me how fragile life is and how little time I spend on relationships." A bridge collapse, a tornado, a bombing, a plane flying into a building, all these tragedies became excuses, he said, "to reach out and connect, to make sense out of life."

Aside from staying away from the investigation scene, or donating blood, or easing the fears of our children, there's not a lot we can do. But we can hold each other at the end of the day, skin to skin or voice to voice or e-mail to e-mail, no matter the distance, no matter how long it's been.

In our little world, that's big comfort.

41 Whose Life is "Good Enough"?

I knew a man who once confessed that he read the obituaries every day—to make sure he wasn't in them. When he died, at age 100, his ruse was up. There he was, displayed prominently with a beautiful tribute to a life well lived, a life that began in Russia and ended in America, a life as an ordinary merchant selling cowboy boots and hand-cranked washing machines in an extraordinary marriage of seventy-six years. A life with two sightings of Halley's comet and thirty-one great-grandchildren.

I confess that I also find my way to the obituaries every day, but not for the same reason. I go because *Entertainment Weekly* only gets me halfway to the answer I seek. I think I've got a handle, now, on how the rich and famous choose to spend their time and trust funds, but the obituary pages are even richer. There, in black and white, is sociological data sufficient for any patient student.

Society, summarized succinctly: The workaholics and tireless volunteers, the billionaires and custodians, the blue-ribbon bakers and golf fanatics. Read the sweet tributes—"She loved her library card and a good game of Scrabble"—and the tragedies that some did not escape: "She was 24." "… after a long and courageous battle with cancer, ALS, depression…"

Some are simply written in code: "He died suddenly."

But, still, there's something missing. The summarizing statement, the grade, if you will, the total points scored on a scale of 1 to 10: Who among them lived the best life? The right life? Who was happiest?

I was struck by this question a few months back when, working a holiday shift in the newsroom, I had to pick between eight outstanding members of the community who would be elevated from paid obituary to recipient of a more fully reported story. The kind of story that shouts: *Read about me. My life meant something beyond the ordinary.*

How would I choose? How could I choose? It felt an awful lot like I was playing God, which seemed like a role better left to, well, God. But a newsroom is filled with testy editors and rigid deadlines and not a lot of time to wax philosophical. I turned to my colleague, Paul: "How do I do this?"

"Just pick what resonates with you."

So I studied the candidates, thought about their families, and waited to *resonate*. "She was active in civic and political affairs, including the Republican Party and Jaycees." "He served in Europe, where he earned a Purple Heart." "She was Miss Minnesota Indian Princess." "He was an accomplished violin player, touring Europe with the Scandinavian Symphony." "He was 21."

I know there is a God, because my shift ended before any decisions had to be made. But a question lingered long after: What about me? Would I make the cut? And, if so, what would I want written?

"She loved coffee and *The Simpsons*, almost as much as she loved her three children ..."

Nah, too glib.

"She ran slowly, typed quickly, and found God in cheesecake." Too blasphemous.

"She never learned how to text-message but she could talk on the phone for three hours without taking a breath." Too true.

"Frankly, she had no idea about a lot of things, but she never stopped searching for answers." There. I like that one.

I'll leave it to my kids to refine the wording, and some editor on a deadline to judge whether it's good enough to reach the bar.

42 Before Grief Goes, Grief Grows

I've seen the trick a hundred times. But there was still something charming about a magician—especially an enthusiastic, underpaid, overdressed county fair magician—stuffing a brightly colored toy into one mystery box, only to have it re-appear (poof!) in another box across the stage.

It was a strange time to be suddenly thinking about grief, no doubt, but I couldn't help myself. Grief has permeated our community for many weeks now. Before we could issue a deep, collective exhale following recovery of the final bridge-collapse victim, we were introduced to the shortened lives of seven others, washed away in torrential flooding in southeastern Minnesota.

"So many lives turned upside down," read one of my newspaper's headlines. At first I stared at it, disoriented, unsure which tragedy it referred to. The bridge? The floods? The miners? Raging, senseless bullets on campus? Facebook suicides?

Such events follow one another like ducks in a gallery, though if we gave each one its due, it would leave us incapable of getting out of bed in the morning.

Until The Worst walks up to our door and knocks, it's our job to keep plugging along, buying groceries, attending PTA meetings, checking in on our elderly parents. The problem is that when such an event strikes *really* close to home, the grief cannot be so easily tossed aside. It's like the toy in that magician's box. Stuff it over here and it reappears over there —poof!

I know a little bit about grief, having lost my father in my twenties. I know even more, though, about what it takes to heal. And I worry that the words we often choose in writing obituaries ("closure" and "healing" being popular choices), while hopeful and well-intended, are simply not true. Closure and healing can take a long, long time.

Beginning Wednesday night at sundown, Jews will begin a ten-day celebration of our New Year. We'll eat apples dipped in honey in hopes that this year will be sweet. We'll toss bread into water as a way to cast away sins. And some of us, on the tenth day, will once again tackle grief.

The service is called *Yizkor*. It's one piece of an intricate structure of mourning practices designed by rabbinic sages. There is *shiva*, the first week after a loved one dies; *shloshim*, the first month; a year of reciting a mourning prayer called the *Kaddish*, then the unveiling of a tombstone at approximately one year. I always thought the timing of this last service brilliantly underscored the fact that we must endure every life-cycle event once without him or her—birthdays, Thanksgiving, a wedding anniversary—before we can even begin to heal.

Yizkor, though, doesn't end. We say it four times a year, for as long as we live, an acknowledgement that mourning is never complete.

When I was a little girl, adults in hushed tones ushered me out of the sanctuary along with other children and non-mourners before *Yizkor* began so as to not tempt the Evil Eye. I don't do the same with my own kids. In fact, I love it when they stand with me to remember the grandfather they know only through photographs and stories. I think it's important for them to see their mother still missing him terribly. It's been nineteen years.

I don't think about him every day. I don't pity myself. I know that there are tragedies far worse, grief far darker. I know this every time I pick up my own newspaper.

Once in a while, though, I'll stop in my tracks, yanked into the past, momentarily disoriented. Poof! I'm ordering an iced coffee, his favorite. Poof! A man wearing a certain cologne rushes past me. Poof! A song. A movie. A laugh. Poof.

We need to keep buying groceries and working our day jobs. But it might be sweet if we remember every so often to look down our row of cubicles, or church pews, or houses, and think about those who still might be missing someone terribly, even after many years. And it might be sweet to simply say, "Tell me your favorite story about him," or "Do you have a photograph of her?"

It's true that we can't always stuff grief back into the box. But when grief reappears (and it will) we can let those who mourn know that we're ready to listen. For as long as it takes.

43 Riding the "Wild Thing"

My friend Robin doesn't take my announcement well. "You did what?" she asks, then turns away, not trying terribly hard to hide the scowl on her face.

Her 10-year-old daughter is considerably more impressed. She pushes me for details: Was I scared? Was it awful? Would I do it again?

Yes. Yes. Probably not, I answer. Quite frankly I, too, am impressed. At 37, I, the responsible one, the un-party girl, have broken free—for three minutes, anyway.

I have ridden the Wild Thing, the scariest rollercoaster in Minnesota.

There's no shortage of speculation among my friends about the motives underlying my decision, though an early midlife crisis and temporary insanity are the most popular theories. How can I tell them the truth? How can I admit that their no-nonsense companion has deliberately, consciously, proposed a bargain to some unseen, unknown power?

"I'll ride this damn thing. You keep my mother alive."

"She can't die," my 7-year-old daughter tells me as I hand her a Popsicle in the kitchen. Her tone is more statement than protest. "Then you wouldn't have any parents."

It's moments like these that remind me how woefully unprepared I am for the task of being anybody's mother. Seven years into parenting and I have far more angst than answers. I decide they should put up a warning sign in maternity wards: BEWARE! YOU THINK YOU KNOW NOTHING ABOUT PARENTING NOW? WAIT UNTIL YOUR CHILDREN START TALKING!

So what do I tell her, this precious, inquisitive child named for my father, who died of cancer ten months before she was born? That just because one person you love dies from cells gone mad doesn't protect you from having to face the possibility again? Is it time to pull out the terribly inadequate parenting speech called "Life's Not Fair"?

Tomorrow, she, her little brother, her father, and I will dress in our best clothes and walk into our synagogue to celebrate the beginning of a new Jewish year. We'll recite the haunting, mantra-like "Unetaneh Tokef," a prayer unique to these special, solemn days of reflection and repentance:

> *On Rosh Hashana it is written and on Yom Kippur*
> *it is sealed . . . who shall live and who shall die, who shall*
> *perish by fire and who by water . . . who by earthquake and*
> *who by plague . . .*

In almost nine hundred years, it has lost neither its relevance nor its intensity. The final message, though, is one of hope—a reminder that there is still a great deal within our control: "But repentance, prayer, and good deeds can annul the severity of the decree."

The uncertainty of the "can" is what worries most of us.

Our small Jewish community is reeling from the loss of six of our children this year alone. One to asthma, another to a brain tumor, a third to a horrible bus accident, another to a motorcycle crash, a fifth to a rare genetic disease. The sixth, a beautiful cadet, dies mysteriously in her sleep. The total of their years is barely more than the life expectancy of one adult. We whisper their names to one another, careful to shield our own children from the brutal truth that what we love can be seized from us in an instant.

But they know.

One morning, just before sunrise, I sneak downstairs into the basement to write at my computer. When I return later to the kitchen, I see my 4-year-old son, gazing out the back window, seated on a stool he has pulled quietly across the kitchen floor. He sits motionless, studying birds in the back yard, his soft back tan, his hair bleached white from a summer in the sun. I wish I had my camera. Then he turns. His eyes are wet. And I realize he hasn't been looking for birds at all. He's been searching for me. I pull him into my arms and nearly smother him in my embrace. "I knew where you were," he assures me, his hot tears running down my neck. "I knew where you were."

My mother calls. She's chucking the chemotherapy. It makes her too sick and, besides, who really knows how much good it'll do anyway? She prefers to believe that the surgery got it all. She wants to live in the present, heal herself with healthy food, long walks and the love of her new husband.

I am furious at her cowardice, until I realize just how brave she is. Unlike me, she doesn't need to bargain with some higher power, doesn't have to stuff herself into a little car for a three-minute almost-kill-me ride at the amusement park. She knows instinctively, through years and loss and holding on, that we can only do so much. Then we simply have to let go, trust, live.

A new year is beginning. And it's impossible to know who shall live and who shall die. So I'll hold on, white-knuckled, to the people I love most, trusting somehow that we'll all be together to recite these prayers again next September.

Because when it comes to the wild thing called life, that's really all I can do.

44 A Long-Buried War Story Hits Home

At twilight on a bone-chilling Christmas Eve 1944, the Belgian transport ship *S. S. Leopoldville* was ferrying American troops toward Cherbourg, France. The former luxury liner had left Southampton, England, around 9 a.m., carrying combat infantry outfits of the 66th Division to fight in the Battle of the Bulge. As Christmas lights glistened in the distance and soldiers sang carols on deck, a German lieutenant in a nearby U-boat sent a torpedo crashing into the ship's side. Hundreds of men were blown apart; hundreds more drowned after being sucked under the ship, or froze in the icy waters of the English Channel. When Christmas morning dawned, more than 800 soldiers were dead—the worst disaster to befall an American infantry division as a result of an enemy submarine attack.

One survivor was a 19-year-old from Omaha, an easygoing kid from an active Presbyterian home who entered the service out of a sense of justice. Now 77 and living in Minneapolis, he only recently felt ready to tell his story by sharing a small piece of it in a holiday memory he sent to the *StarTribune*.

He could not have known how deeply I wanted to hear it. That's because there was another man on that ship, a 19-year-old Jewish soldier from Paterson, N.J., who chose never to speak of that night to his children. When he died at age 63, those memories died with him.

That man was my father.

"You've got to read this one."

Every December, the *StarTribune* solicits stories from readers for a Holiday Giving feature. Warm stories pour in about kindnesses from strangers and loved ones. Truth is, I don't read them all. But when Henry Andersen's story crossed my colleague's desk, she was genuinely moved and passed it along to me. I read every word.

"My particular troopship, *Leopoldville III* . . . ," Andersen wrote. My father's ship.

I knew that my father had been awarded a Purple Heart for what he endured that night, but as a child, I never understood the magnitude of the loss, and he never found the words to tell me. Only once did he speak of it, to my mother on Christmas night 1953, the year they were married. He startled her as he sat in the bathtub and she stood at the bathroom sink of their first apartment in Detroit. In a hushed voice, he told her that he was forever haunted by the memory of swimming in the English Channel, loaded down with field gear, toward a piece of wood, and reaching it before another soldier could.

"I wanted to live," he told my mother (she all of 21), his grief sudden and raw. He was in the water for nearly an hour before being pulled to safety by a French fishing vessel.

I made a copy of Andersen's note and took it home. That night, I reached for a book my mother had sent me, a book I'd been meaning to read for three years—*S.S. Leopoldville*

Disaster, by Allan Andrade. I knew that my father's name was listed in the back under "Survivors." Sgt. Henry William Andersen was there, too. Both served in weapons platoons, Andersen in Company E, my father in Company L.

With my 11-year-old son sitting next to me on the bed, I made the phone call. "Mr. Andersen, I'd like to tell you about an amazing coincidence," I said.

Two days later, I was sitting in the living room of the Andersens' apartment in downtown Minneapolis. Henry (Hank) Andersen is, at 77, a gregarious man, a natty dresser and still quite a looker. He stands 6 feet 3 (down from his youthful high of 6-5) and remains a trim 170 pounds. He has silver hair, sky-blue eyes, ski-slope cheekbones (courtesy of his Danish roots), and a deep, comforting voice that served him well during his forty years as a Presbyterian minister. He wears hearing aids because of partial hearing loss he suffered as a mortar sergeant.

The apartment he shares with his wife, Mary, is filled with religious art, as well as keepsakes of his experiences in the war nearly sixty years ago, including several books about the Leopoldville disaster, Army photographs, and his khaki Eisenhower jacket. It still fits.

Sidney Rosenblum and Hank Andersen were born in 1925, and the Depression hit their families hard. Andersen's father took off every day at 4:30 a.m. from their home in Omaha, peddling eggs, Wonder bread, and vegetables from nearby farmers' markets. He'd return home for dinner, resting only on Sundays. His mother balanced homemaking with community activism as president of the Nebraska Gladiolus Society and substitute violinist in the Omaha Symphony.

Andersen played clarinet and saxophone in the high school marching band and formed his own dance band, Hank's Hep-cats, which played at school dances on Friday afternoons.

My father liked to say his Russian immigrant parents were so poor they couldn't afford to give him a middle name. Like Andersen, he found joy in music. By 10, he was singing at weddings and bar mitzvahs, earning as much as $10 for "Oh Promise Me." He promptly gave the money to his parents. He became a student cantor and starred in school musicals.

He and Andersen were called to duty at age 18. Both were smart and tall, and both were quickly promoted to sergeant. "They liked big guys to give orders," Andersen said.

At about 2 a.m. on Dec. 24, 1944, Andersen and my father were among more than 2,200 troops from the 262nd and 264th regiments called to emergency duty in the Battle of the Bulge. It would be the largest land battle of World War II, and would ultimately decide the fate of Nazi Germany. Andersen remembers the frenzied atmosphere that morning.

"It was a miserable day," he said. "Cold, rainy, dark." Soldiers boarded the *Leopoldville* for the nine-hour ride, "tumbling over one another. Officers couldn't even get a list together of who was on the boat."

Cargo space had been converted into troop compartments to accommodate more than twice the number of soldiers than the ship was designed to carry. Aisles between tiers were crammed with packs, rifles, duffel bags and steel helmets. Life jackets had been issued haphazardly, if at all, and without instruction. There was nothing to eat but uncooked K-rations, hard cheese, and chocolate bars.

Around 9 a.m., the 501-foot, 11,500-ton transport ship pulled away from dock and led a convoy into the English Channel. Five and a half miles outside Cherbourg, just before 6 p.m., Andersen noticed a heaviness overtaking the soldiers. Many were seasick, and many were despondent as they glimpsed Christmas lights in the distance and thought of how far they were from home. He called to his squad: "Come on, guys! It's Christmas Eve!"

Twenty or thirty men followed Andersen down to the hold to serenade their fellow soldiers with boisterous carols: "God Rest Ye Merry, Gentlemen," "We Three Kings of Orient Are," "Hark! The Herald Angels Sing."

As the men moved back up to the deck, their voices rose, and dozens of other soldiers joined them until nearly 200 were singing. Andersen does not recall meeting my father, nor does he know for sure whether my father was on deck when the torpedo hit. But he believes that he was.

"There was nowhere else to go," he said. "That's where the focus was."

I believe he was there, too. It is no stretch to picture the man who loved to sing joining in this inspirational moment. And it would explain something I've always wondered about, something that has been the inspiration for great ribbing by my friends: I'm a Jewish girl who loves Christmas music. I no longer have to wonder why. Christmas carols probably saved my father's life.

The torpedo hit just after 6 p.m. in the bottom stern section of the ship, blowing a huge hole in the hull. Andersen's first memory as the ship trembled was of a geyser shooting skyward. The lights went out, the ship began to list. Andersen watched the Belgian crewmen and the ship's first mate rush to lower two of the precious few lifeboats.

"We thought they were for us," he said. "Then the crew jumped in them and bid us farewell."

As soldiers screamed for their lives, Andersen did the only thing he could think to do. He kept singing. "God Rest Ye Merry, Gentlemen," "We Three Kings of Orient Are" and "Hark! The Herald Angels Sing." His booming voice rang out. Those carols, he said, "were my lifeline."

As the ship began to sink, a British destroyer in the convoy, the *H.M.S. Brilliant*, pulled up next to the much larger *Leopoldville* to rescue what soldiers they could. Many did not jump far enough and were crushed between the two ships as horrified shipmates watched. Others, including my father, spilled into the water.

Andersen looked around at the men of Company E. "They had frozen. No one would jump. I thought, `Hey, buddy, you're the sergeant. You have to move.' Instinctively, I got up on the rail. The destroyer was coming up on the rail. Our ship was coming down. I jumped."

He made it, and slid across the deck. He helped two or three others across before passing out.

He awoke on the floor of a Cherbourg maritime station on Christmas morning, uninjured. Andersen then told me the story that he originally sent to the *StarTribune*. It was the only time in three hours of talking that his voice broke and he cried.

Black quartermaster troops stationed in Cherbourg and segregated from white troops offered survivors their Christmas dinner. Andersen, too grief-stricken to think of eating, didn't want to go, but an order was an order. Soon, two ½-ton trucks came to pick up the men and take them to the black troops' stationing area.

"As we lined up for their dinner, gradually the entire quartermaster outfit surrounded us and began singing Christmas carols, gently, softly, magnificently."

A strange and profound feeling swept over him. "In sorrow and wonder," said Andersen, his voice breaking, "we began to sing with them."

The music, he said, gave him sustenance to go on, something to believe in. "Health. Hope. Comfort. Peace. When I left that place, I was healed."

My father was discharged in April 1946, Andersen a few weeks later. Both were awarded Purple Hearts, and both went on to marry and raise children into adulthood. Both chose careers in healing professions, hoping their work could, in part, help them understand the darkest side of human nature and the capacity to overcome it. Andersen had planned to become a lawyer. Instead, he graduated from the McCormick Seminary, now affiliated with the University of Chicago, and spent nearly forty years as a minister in Kansas, Chicago, and Cleveland. He and Mary moved to Minneapolis to be near their son Tim Hart-Andersen, senior pastor of Westminster Presbyterian Church in downtown Minneapolis, and his family. They have three other children and nine grandchildren.

After the war, my father turned down a role in a traveling Broadway production and completed his bachelor's degree in psychology, a field he would revel in for more than thirty years.

He had not an ounce of bitterness when, at 63, he developed inoperable cancer. He had already cheated death once.

Andersen says he is still haunted by a question that he knows has no answer. "I'm puzzled why I survived and why many, many didn't," he said. Every Christmas, he relives that question, finding strength in faith and family.

There is a Yiddish word, *besheret*, which means something that was meant to be. Before leaving the Andersens last week, I was filled with gratitude but still felt my visit unfinished. We had looked through every book but one, and I realized that I had come for more than stories. I reached for what looked like a high school yearbook, musty and tattered with age. On the cover was written "The Black Panther: 66th Division." The pages were divided by companies, but there were no names under photographs of the young men.

With Mary's help, I searched the section marked "Company E" and there, second row down on the right, sixth photograph over, was her Hank, movie-star handsome, the happy-go-lucky kid from Omaha. I turned a few pages to Company L. And, of course, there he was, in the same position on his page that Andersen was on his, second row down on the right, sixth photograph over, the singing kid from Paterson, cap tilted almost too far to the side, ears protruding, with the playful smile of someone who could not have imagined what he was about to see.

On Dec. 24, 1944, the troopship *S.S. Leopoldville* left Southampton, England, and set out for Cherbourg, France. Hundreds of soldiers—boys really—would perish in the icy waters as their families back home sang Christmas carols and awaited word of their return. One who survived couldn't tell the story of that night. But with the healing touch of time, and a healthy dose of *besheret,* another could. Neither ever forgot what he was given that night, nor what he should work for in his life. Health. Hope. Comfort. Peace.

In this season, and in every other, there is really nothing more they could ask.

IV. HOLIDAYS AND HOLY…DAZE

45 Holiday Letter (WON'T BE SENDING)

Dearest (a) loved ones and friends (b) mere acquaintances:

It's been another (a) glorious (b) disastrous year!

Here's a rundown of (a) highlights (b) every deadly detail of how we spent 2002: If (a) it's not nearly enough (b) you have suicidal tendencies, do check out our family Web site, http://www.ourextraordinaryfamily.com, which is filled with photographs of (a) our exotic, expensive vacations on three continents (b) our stockbroker under his bed in the fetal position.

—Timmy was (again!) the top seller in his third-grade classroom's fall fundraiser, selling a whopping 350 (a) chocolate bars (b) Ritalin tablets. He was voted room representative to the student council for his prowess in (a) leadership (b) Yu-Gi-Oh! Timmy, (a) a straight-A student (b) a 15-year-old who still can't read, spends his free time (a) volunteering at the local animal shelter (b) kicking cats. He is still hoping to become (a) a brain surgeon (b) an adult.

—Suzeeey began (a) kindergarten (b) body piercing this year, and has dazzled her Montessori teachers with her ability to (a) solve complex math equations using lima beans (b) sweep the floor with her lengthy eyelashes. Suzeeey (a) takes dance lessons, plays classical piano, heals the sick, goes to bed when asked (b) talks back to her parole officer and is looking forward to becoming (a) a United Nations peace negotiator (b) a lawyer so she can sue us.

—Rick (a) seized the opportunity to chase his dreams (b) got his butt fired and is now enjoying weekly meetings with (a) a certified life coach (b) a certified drunk. After 15 years of marriage, we can honestly say that we've never been (a) happier (b) more certain we made the wrong choice.

—The year's highlight for me was (a) I turned 40 (b) I turned the mattresses, and have never felt more (a) focused (b) forgetful. For my birthday, I treated myself to (a) hot-rocks massage (b) hot flashes that could melt chocolate, and am seriously considering using my MBA to (a) open a Parisienne-style coffeehouse (b) get a minimum-wage job at Starbucks.

As this year comes to an end, we wish you and yours (a) a joyful and peaceful holiday season (b) would stop calling us for favors.

(a) Until next year (b) If you're lucky

Gail

46 The Five Stages of a Family Holiday

I: ANTICIPATION

Characterized by: Excitement, optimism, warm feelings of familial love, a touch of amnesia.

Telltale signs: Sparkling kitchen counters; refrigerator stuffed with turkey, roast beef, Swedish meatballs; photos of each family member dredged out of the basement and strategically placed on entry-room credenza.

Duration: Begins when invitations are e-mailed; ends when first guests arrive with feverish baby, yapping dog and tofu lasagna.

II: APPREHENSION

Characterized by: Stomach cramps, quick peek at family photos to make sure those arriving are the right people.

Telltale signs: Your mother starts in on your weight gain. Mother-in-law asks whether you really meant to use paper napkins. Ten-year-old niece asks when she can watch her *8 Mile* DVD. Sister starts up video of recent

Caribbean cruise. Brother doesn't show. Dad's new girlfriend does. Mom reminds you that she is allergic to dogs - and to Dad.

Duration: The longest 15 minutes of your life.

III: CHAOS

Characterized by: Turf wars over gravy. And over when to sit down for dinner. And who has to sit on the piano bench. And whether the TV should be on or off during dinner. And when dessert should be served. And whether Rice Dream can be deemed a real dessert. Mom says her throat is closing up. Dad says that sounds promising. Baby demonstrates that she is not finished with projectile vomiting. Dog pulls turkey off table. Vegetarians applaud.

Telltale signs: Smoke alarm goes off, but you refuse to pull your head out of the oven until they all go away.

Duration: Well, since childhood really.

IV: ACCEPTANCE

Characterized by: A calm feeling suddenly washing over you.

Telltale signs: You find yourself sitting on the couch, eating five pieces of pie and listening to Uncle Fred tell you it's time you developed a sound financial planning strategy. Why not? Your

7-year-old is watching *8 Mile* with her cousins because your opinion no longer matters and that's OK.
Duration: Until the Paxil runs out.

V: EUPHORIA

Characterized by: Tears of joy
Telltale signs: You stop daydreaming long enough to notice that your mother, mother-in-law, sister and Dad's girlfriend have cleaned up the entire kitchen. The baby and dog are playing on the floor. The men are dozing. The cousins have shifted to watching *Finding Nemo*.
Duration: One year exactly, at which point these same people will arrive at your house again. Because you are family. And you love them, despite yourself.

47 A Jewish Girl's Take On Christmas

"M erry Christmas!" the bell ringer shouted as we folded a dollar bill into his kettle last week.

"Merry Christmas!" I shouted back. And then I began to count. Two, three, four, fi....

"We should wear a Jewish star," my 7-year-old daughter said, waiting longer than I'd expected. "Then he'd know we don't celebrate Christmas."

She's our youngest child, hence the last one to make peace with December, the month of magic and merriment that stops at her front door.

I can recite my parenting speech in my sleep, and probably do: "Yes, love, I know you want a Christmas tree. But we're Jewish. We have our own special holidays."

She's not buying it. I didn't buy it when I was 7, either. Back then, I stood in front of a mammoth Christmas tree in my classroom, holding a tiny gold menorah and recounting to my classmates the tale of a Jewish victory for religious freedom more than two thousand years ago. They were bored until I got to the eight days—eight gifts part. That perked them up.

But even then, before it was government-sanctioned or politically correct, my parents endorsed a pluralistic approach. Every Christmas morning, I crossed the street to my best friend Laura's house to play Santa and hand out presents.

In turn, she and her sisters came over to light candles on Hanukkah, to play dreidel, a spinning top game, and eat oil-drenched potato pancakes.

I learned not to fear differences, but to appreciate them. I learned to ask questions and forgive myself if my questions made people laugh: "Does Santa have a regular job?"

I learned more about my own history, too, because people were genuinely interested. Still are.

In fact, my biggest challenge is trying to keep my Christian friends from straining as they perform Cirque de Soleil-worthy acrobatics to assure that my family feels included. They sing "Oh, Dreidel, Dreidel, Dreidel," invite us to "holiday" parties, and send pretty Hanukkah cards. Honestly, I wish they wouldn't. Yes, Hanukkah is a holiday, but a minor one, the kind Jews celebrate every few weeks around the calendar.

I can't speak for my fellow Jews (wouldn't dare, actually) but I'd rather my Christian neighbors enjoy their wondrous Christmas without worrying about me. Wish me "Merry Christmas" and I'll return the greeting, or at least smile. I'm happy to come to your Christmas party and admire your Christmas tree.

I don't want my children to have to stand in front of a Christmas tree in their public school as their father and I did, but I won't stop shopping at Target if they call a sale a Christmas sale. (Actually, I can't think of anything that would keep me away from Target).

I've made peace with December as a minority in a predominately Christian culture. It's my job to help my children make peace with it, too.

These days, all I want for Christmas is for this phony, ugly, made-up controversy surrounding it to stop. There is no attack on Christmas, nothing insidious seeping into the water while we sleep. All I see everywhere I turn are people trying to do the right thing. The harpist in the bank who played a lively medley of Jewish music for us. The shopping mall Santa who caught my eye as we walked quickly past and whispered to my kids, "Tell your mom I'm tired of sitting on my *tuchas* (rear end)."

My husband's grandfather would have loved that one. Jack Gurwitz, who lived to 100, was born in the Russian shtetl, living under the daily weight of poverty and pogroms. Once, soldiers burst into his classroom demanding to arrest Yakov Gurevitch. They left shortly after because Yakov was 4 years old and barefoot. Decades later Yakov, now Jack, emigrated to America and opened a dry goods store in tiny Three Rivers, Texas. Every Sunday, Jack and his wife, Sarah, placed their children on the train for a 200-mile round-trip ride for a Jewish education in San Antonio. And every December in Three Rivers, ringing up Victrolas or rugged Levis, Jack and Sarah wished their customers a heartfelt Merry Christmas. They knew who they were, where they came from, and the kind of people they wanted to be. I want the same for my family.

And the same for yours.

48 Camp Is For Letting Go

O ur youngest child returns next Sunday from her first overnight camp experience. Two weeks of swimming, singing, goopy pancakes the size of her head, crushes on cute counselors, new best friends. But I have a feeling that her first words to me when she steps off the bus won't be about any of those things. I'm betting on something closer to: "You didn't e-mail me! Not even once!"

It's true. I didn't e-mail her. Not even once. I find myself once again on the Bad Mom end of things, but I remain an old-fashioned summer camp snob. Just because the darling, desperately loved child now can receive daily e-mails from her parents doesn't mean she should. (For the record, I never view the photographs posted on the camp website, either.)

Please allow me to explain. When I went to music camp in the Jemez Mountains of New Mexico as a kid, there was something called a "letter." It arrived not nearly often enough because I, being a homesick sort of child, only allowed my parents to ship me off in one-week increments. I was lucky to receive one letter at camp before it was time to go home to be bored for the rest of the summer.

There was one year, though, when I unwisely shared with my parents the news that any child who received more than seven letters in one day would be commanded to stand on a wooden table in the mess hall in front of the entire camp contingent and sing a song. My parents did a gotcha and sent me seven letters in one day. I sang "Happy Birthday."

Mostly, though, summer after summer I cherished those spectacular white envelopes that arrived sparingly with my name written in Mom's or Dad's handwriting. I'd sit in my top bunk at quiet time in the afternoon, the smell of pine or rain wafting through the cabin window, and I'd devour every word. Suddenly, my parents' lives were interesting. Who knew?

This, I am convinced, is the point of summer camp. Not to discover that your parents have lives, but to spend a few days apart from their lives. During that interval, you may discover that you have a life, too. Summer camp is a chance to explore what independence feels like in new but safe surroundings. It grants our children an opportunity to stretch, try new roles, eat new foods, cry and get over it, feel the fear and freedom of not having their parents or other significant grownups hovering nearby. It's the chance to ache with longing for home until you think you might die, and then, a day or two later, find yourself begging your parents to let you stay another week. (Well, that's what I did.)

Summer camp is our kids' practice run at separating from us, something they're going to have to get good at before we take down the Hannah Montana posters and start hauling exercise machines and workstations into their bedrooms. But they won't feel that separation so strongly if they get e-mails from us every day or imagine that we're watching their every move on digital camera.

So when a friend asked me last week if I'd been monitoring

my neophyte camper's activities via the web, or shooting off daily e-mails, I think I surprised him with my answer. Um, no, I said. But I did write my daughter a few riveting letters.

And I never worried about whether she was OK. Not even once.

49 The Summer Check-off List

Heard on the radio the other day that temps were going to dip into the 50s for a few nights. Already! Time to reach into the sweater box, I guess. Time, too, to reach for The List.

I have made The List for 14 years now, 14 years being how long I have lived in Minnesota; the list being my favorite, and most therapeutic, summer activity.

Before moving here, I lived only in hot-weather spots where nobody had any idea when to store their white pumps. Where I never had to dread passing a well-meaning neighbor on a beautiful summer day musing: "Hard to believe we'll likely have snow in three months, yah?"

And so, The List! A compilation of what I simply *must* do if I hope to have any peace of mind come Labor Day. My summer is not complete until I:

- Ride the Lake Harriet trolley. When my two children grew older and thought the idea a bore, I did what any self-respecting mother would do: I had another baby. Carly, 4, and I have ridden the trolley two times already this summer. No, make that three.

- Eat Minnesota sweet corn. The makeshift stand appeared magically in a nearby parking lot earlier this month:

Sweet corn! I almost cried, which means one of two things: I have a pathetic little life and perhaps should not be admitting it here. Or the corn is really quite good.

- Visit the cabin. Impressive, yes? Transplant learns how to become a true Minnesotan with a cabin up north! Actually, I became a dear friend to a Minnesotan with a cabin up north. All the fishing, water-skiing, loon-spotting, shopping, and sleeping in a hammock one could hope for. None of the property taxes.

- See fireworks. In a wonderfully lucky twist of fate, July Fourth falls in the summer—every year! My need to see fireworks goes beyond amusement and falls squarely into the category called "obsession." Kin who would rather not stay up that late stay up anyway. Momma says. I have dragged my family to the shores of Stillwater, propped them up on the car's hood at a gas station in Brainerd, oohed and aahed from a boat in Ely, leaned against somebody's tree in south Minneapolis and sat precariously atop a wall near the Stone Arch bridge to enjoy the sparkling glory. My 10-year-old son suggested that, with new fireworks laws in place, he'll present a dazzling back-yard display next year. (I told him I'd get back to him on that.)

- Stroll the Aquatennial sand sculptures. I'm drawn each year to Lake Calhoun's Thomas Beach on the final Sunday of the Aquatennial. There's something poetic about people willing to create wonder from sand and water, knowing that it will not last for posterity—or even overnight.

- Take a family vacation. I mean the old-fashioned kind: by car. These vacations, where children develop clever new ways to torture one another, where stomachs ache and Gameboys break, will metamorphose into the happiest memories we have as adults. Promise.

- Eat my husband's pesto. I almost resisted adding this one—not because his pesto isn't fab, and not out of embarrassment that two of my entries have to do with eating, but because hubby rolls his eyes at my summer list. Still, it really isn't summer until he and the kids go into the garden and bring back a handful of sweet, pungent basil, mix it with pine nuts, garlic, olive oil, butter, more butter and fresh grated Parmesan cheese, and offer it up to be eaten—make that inhaled—with a salad and fresh bread.

Our latest batch came not a minute too soon. On the morning after our most recent pesto feast, little Carly stood at the top porch step and refused to walk down until I got her a sweater.

I grabbed one without panicking. Autumn, come if you must! I've checked The List. And I am ready.

MY EX'ES KILLER BLENDO PESTO

(Enough for about 6 servings of pasta)

2 cups fresh basil leaves (see note below)
½ cup olive oil
2 Tbls pine nuts
2 cloves garlic, lightly crushed with a heavy knife
       handle and peeled
1 t salt
½ cup freshly grated Parmesan cheese
2 Tbls freshly grated Romano pecorino cheese
3 Tbls butter, softened to room temperature

1. Put the basil, olive oil, pine nuts, garlic cloves, and salt in the blender and mix at high speed. Stop from time to time and scrape the ingredients down toward the bottom of the blender cup with a rubber spatula.

2. When the ingredients are evenly blended, pour into a bowl and beat in the two grated cheeses by hand. (This is not much work, and it results in a more interesting texture and better flavor than you get when you mix in the cheese in the blender.) When the cheese has been evenly incorporated into the other ingredients, beat in the softened butter.

3. Before spooning the pesto over pasta, add to it a tablespoon or so of the hot water in which the pasta has boiled.

50 Beyond the Bucket List

My new "1,000 Places to See Before You Die" calendar has been sitting on my desk for two weeks, waiting to be hung. The photos are huge and luscious and, in the dead of winter, who wouldn't want to gaze upon an Amalfi Coast sunset or fantasize about shooting the rapids in Banff National Park?

Well, me. I know I'm supposed to feel inspired by this growing family of products promoting the world's wonders. But I just feel tired. Anybody out there want to join my club, where our highest aspiration before we die is to max out our 401(k)'s?

There was a time when I actually enjoyed this gimmick. Just a few years ago, I could buy books and calendars with titles such as "50 Places to See Before You Die." Fifty places! Quite a stretch considering my current years on the planet, but even choosing 10 among them would seem a victory.

Then things got nutty. Fifty places became 100. One hundred places to see—and things to do—grew to 365, which leaped to 1,000 and then ... 1,001. (What, I wonder, was the one they added? Someplace easy to overlook, like China?)

Now even the last bastion of escapism—the movies—is getting into the act. Jack Nicholson and Morgan Freeman's characters in *The Bucket List* are dying. So, they're doing what any of us would do in that situation: leaping out of prop planes, racing vintage cars, and dropping in at the Taj Mahal. Check. Check. Check.

I know. I'm being too literal. No one really expects us to become uber-adventurers, especially we Americans with our drooping dollar and comparatively paltry number of vacation days. But we're human, after all, and it's hard to look at such enticements without feeling a bit like a loser for never having cruised the Ayeyarwady (it's in Myanmar—I looked it up).

The bigger problem (aside from shelling out twenty bucks to be reminded that I'll be six feet under before I know it) is that I've seen what happens to people who try too hard to check Great Experiences off a list. They get cranky, even in spectacular places.

I once saw a couple step off a train in glorious, on-everyone's-list Paris. He was several steps behind her, pulling their overpacked luggage. "Yes," he said, rolling his eyes, "that's because you are always right."

Yikes. Too much pressure, if you ask me, to have the times of their lives. I just hope they only bought the "50 Places" book.

So, let's leave them to their lists. We'll make our own. Let's call ours "1,000 Moments of Serendipity." No, let's be daring: 1,001!

Because the best moments are almost always the least expected or planned, aren't they? Snow days. A lifelong friendship made on a city bus. A meteor sighting on your first date. A teacher's observation that turns our lives in a fortuitous direction. Raindrops dancing on a tent. Winning the door prize. A teenager admitting that you, Mom, were right. OK, I'm still waiting for that one, but I am certain it would make my list.

I don't mean we shouldn't dream. I just think we should keep our bucket list small. Throw in one or two places we hunger to experience and, then, for goodness' sake, make it happen.

Meanwhile, we can keep our senses open to the potential thousands of unanticipated joys and thrills that can come our way if we're paying attention. Right here, where we live.

If we're racing cars, we might be moving too fast to notice.

In Conclusion: Stuff I've Learned

Coping skills from my house to your house for the price of this book.

Looking back, it's clear that I Did Not Learn Everything I Ever Needed to Know in Kindergarten. The only thing I learned in kindergarten is that the teacher didn't take kindly to kids who peed on their carpet square. My education in how to get along with my fellow humans began in earnest a bit later and, frankly, continues to this day.

But after fifty-plus years on this planet, I've collected plenty of coping strategies that may make me look wiser than I am. This could explain why, when it comes to advice, I'm rarely on the receiving end anymore, but often in the role of "doling out." I'm more than happy to oblige. I even take my own advice on occasion.

So here you go, glorious readers—you who have hung in with me to the end of this book. I am so filled with gratitude that if I still hired babysitters I'd share their phone numbers with you. If I baked, I'd give you a prized, secret family recipe. I would.

But for now, these choice morsels will just have to do.

When You're Worried About Something, Ask Yourself: "What's The Worst Thing That Could Happen?"

My very wise father, Sidney Rosenblum, of blessed memory, taught me this one. It's my favorite coping tool. I've used it for big stuff and little stuff. I'm stuck in traffic and will be late for a meeting (little stuff). I'm going to lose my job (bigger). Someone I love is dying (really big). Go on. Ask: "What is the worst thing that could happen?" Answering candidly can be hard, scary, or incredibly sad. But facing our fears jolts us awake so we can plan our next move.

You know that popular saying: "We're never given more than we can handle?" I hate that popular saying. The universe throws all sorts of crap at us that we're not ready to handle. I don't like "Everything happens for a reason," either. Horrible things happen that are terribly unfair. But in our darkest hour, people come out of the woodwork to help us, if we let them. The worst thing that could happen? To shut ourselves off from them.

3-2-1

I number myself among those who truly believe in taking the high road—where, by the way, you can always find a parking space, since so few people go there. So you may be surprised to learn that I am also a big supporter of kvetching, complaining, whining, pillow-punching, etc. But at a certain point, you've got to stop all that. This is where the 3-2-1 rule comes in.

Here's how it works. Take your current frustration (your spouse just insulted you, you screwed up in a meeting, you forgot to pay a bill and now you owe a late fee...) and assign it 1, 2 or 3, based on just how many days you want to get tied up in knots about it. For all the above, I'd say one day is plenty, but, hey, it's your screw-up. This means that you get one glorious day to OBSSESS about it. You don't have to stuff it, or pretend you're not pissed off, hurt, or embarrassed. You get to lick your wounds like a war martyr. For one day. Then you have to give it up already. Bigger stuff gets two days. Or three. I swear this works. I'm on Day Three as I write this, and in a few hours I'm going to have to let go of something and I am really, really, almosttttttttttttttttttttttt ready. Really. I'm going to stop. I am.

SHOOT FOR 80 PERCENT.

This is my rip-off of the 80-20 rule used by business executives, a rule I don't really understand because I stink at math. Not only am I giving up on perfection, I don't even VALUE perfection (as if). I now shoot for 80 percent in pretty much everything. Do I give my kids 80 percent of my attention when I'm with them? Do I do the same at work? (hoping at this moment that my bosses have missed this section?) Were my brownies a solid B? Do I eat well 80 percent of the time (brownies excluded)? Good enough is finally, blessedly, good enough for me. (Cue the violins). The biggest payoff? I get a lot more stuff done. Just please don't ask for that increase as a percentage.

Ask Yourself: "What If I'm Wrong About That?"

Here's a secret: I know *exactly* what other people are thinking (it's a gift!!!) except when I'm wrong or mostly wrong. That happens a lot. To heal myself, I've started using a revolutionary approach. I ask. I say something like this: "Hey, I can't read your mind. I'd love to know what you're thinking, if you're willing to tell me."

I still screw up, guess wrong, get anxious sometimes. Here's an example of what NOT to do:

— My boyfriend Patrick: "Is that a new color of lipstick? It's pink. You don't usually wear pink."
— Me: (All the following dialogue is in my head): "He doesn't like my pink lipstick. No, it's worse! He doesn't like me! He wants to break up! I'm going to die alone! I'm going to become a hoarder of jelly jars, with 27 cats! I should just..."
— Patrick: "I like it."
— Me: "You like it?"

Never Exaggerate Your Own Importance.

Don't worry too much about what everyone is thinking about you. Honestly? They're NOT thinking about you.

Ask The Stupid Question.

People are so grateful. Really. Either they, too, want to know the answer, or they know the answer and can feel superior. Everybody wins!

Buy Your Own Flowers.

Waiting for someone to buy you flowers can leave you waiting...and waiting.... S/he loves you, s/he doesn't love you. Maybe. But maybe s/he just wants to show you love in a different way. You want flowers? Pick out exactly the ones you want, take them home and put them in a beautiful vase.

N.N.I.
(Also Known As "No New Information.")

You may have noticed by now that human relationships, while being essential to our happiness and survival, are also often a pain in the ass. Sometimes, you desperately want people to do the right thing and, guess what? They don't! They can't apologize or ask for forgiveness. They can't pick up the slack, or their underwear, they just can't, and you can knock your head against the wall for a long, long time and nothing will change.

This doesn't mean that nothing will ever change. I've seen people change in amazing ways. But, right now, in this moment, you are getting NNI: No New Information. Instead of expending your valuable time and energy fretting again (and again), just say, "No New Information," let it go and move on. When there IS new information, you'll know.

When You Have To Choose Between Being Right And Being Kind, Choose Kind.

I can't think of anything else to say about this one.

Don't Push Send.

Wait 24 hours. For the record, I'm still working on this one myself.

'Because It Matters'

Yes, he makes that idiotic request for you to please load the dishwasher with the forks up. And, yes, she'd like you to please stop throwing a wet towel on the bed, when it's just not that big of a deal. Crazy-making requests? Absolutely. Do them anyway. I mean it. Do them anyway. Here's the reason: *Because it matters to him or her.* These requests may seem small or stupid to you, but to the person you love, honoring them means you are listening, and that is a wonderful way to show love. Um, you are listening, right?

Go To Bed.

This is for those of you plagued by the primarily female disease called, "I'm-going-to-pack-one-more-lunch-send-one-more-e-mail-throw-in-one-more-load-of-laundry-even-though-I-am-getting-progressively-more-insanely-bitchy...." Stop. Don't do it. Everything will go faster, and smoother, in the morning. And, while we're on the subject...

Go To Bed Angry.

I know. You're never supposed to go to bed angry. What happens, then, is that you stay up all night fighting. This is a good idea...how? I say, go to bed (see above). Every challenge, and everybody who causes them, can be managed with more grace and dignity after a good night's sleep.

TRY HARDER.

I once had a therapist I loved so much that I started making up shit about my life so I could keep seeing her. Eventually she was on to me, and graciously fired me. I still miss her. One of my favorite moments, though, came when I was complaining about a particularly difficult passage in a relationship and was looking to her for validation to jump ship. She leaned toward me and said, "I don't usually give advice to my clients, but I'm going to give it to you." And then she said two simple words: *Try harder.*

Try harder? Yep, that's really what she said. So I did. And I am really glad that I did.

NO ONE EVER REALLY GROWS UP.

I've been living with, loving and loathing, interviewing and interacting with people for a long, long time now and, frankly, I've come to realize that we're all still infants. Much of the time, no matter how dressed up we get, we still feel small and frightened and inadequate and hungry for something (food, love, sex, warmth, acceptance). I've seen elderly women struggle mightily after a falling out with a friend. I've talked with men at the end of their careers who feel marginalized and dejected. We feel so deeply all the days of our lives—if we're lucky. So when we bump up against other people at work or play or on the freeway, there is something very grown-up we can do.

Try harder.

About the Author

Gail Rosenblum is a columnist for the Minneapolis *Star Tribune*, writing two to three columns a week on current issues, trends and the complexities of human relationships. Gail joined the *Star Tribune* in 2000 as Variety Team Leader, and returned to full-time writing in 2005, covering the unique "relationships" beat. She was named a columnist in 2009. Before coming to the *Star Tribune*, Gail worked for nearly twenty years as a reporter, editor and essayist for many newspapers and national magazines, including *Sesame Street Parents*, *Parents Magazine* and *Child*. She has a bachelor's degree in journalism from the University of New Mexico and a master's degree in journalism, with a concentration in public health, from the University of Minnesota. Her writing has garnered awards from the Associated Press, American Association of Sunday and Feature Editors, and the Society of Professional Journalists in Minnesota and Texas. Gail is the mother of three children.

Visit her on-line at *www.gailrosenblum.com*.